HARDPRESS.NET
HOME OF HARD-TO-FIND BOOKS

Essay on the Nature and Perpetuity of the Office of the Primitive Evangelist
by David Douglas (Of Hamsterley.)

Address:
HardPress
8345 NW 66TH ST #2561
MIAMI FL 33166-2626
USA
Email: info@hardpress.net

MATTHEW MALCOLM

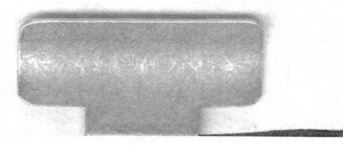

35

ESSAY

ON THE

NATURE AND PERPETUITY

OF

THE OFFICE

OF THE

PRIMITIVE EVANGELIST.

BY

DAVID DOUGLAS,

PASTOR OF THE BAPTIST CHURCH, HAMSTERLEY, DURHAM.

" To suppose, that our Lord Jesus Christ has commanded his church to teach all nations, without affording the means of obeying this command, would be highly profane. There is this power some where: Where is it?

WARD's *Farewell Letters.*

LONDON:

THOMAS WARD & CO.,

PATERNOSTER ROW.

1838.

T. H. CLARK,
PRINTER,
NEWCASTLE-ON-TYNE

PREFACE.

ONE part of the title of this small volume is very likely to beget suspicion in the minds of some who may glance at it. It has so long been regarded as a settled point by most, that the evangelist's office was extraordinary and temporary, that for any one now to affirm that such is not the case, is a circumstance adapted to lay him open to the suspicion that he is some deluded fanatic of a certain school that have, of late, attempted to revive, not only all the primitive offices, but all the primitive gifts. To shield himself against such an imputation, the writer, in his title page, has taken refuge under a name that will be little suspected of heresy. The venerated name of Ward, in connexion with the ideas contained in the sentence cited from him, will surely, in some degree, rescue him from the suspicion of fanaticism, and, perhaps, induce the reader of the title page, to read both the preface and the work itself. If so, perhaps, his feelings may be still more conciliated, when he is reminded of another remark of the same distinguished individual. That remark is, " The offices of apostles and prophets have ceased in the church, if the word prophets, in Eph. iv. 11, signify those who interpreted the discourses delivered in an unknown tongue. But where is the next order, evangelists, and why are pastors, or teachers, the only order left ?   Does not this simple fact supply the testimony of volumes, and prove that our churches have lost sight of the great object of their existence?"*   Here, then, is surely something like a con_viction of the perpetuity of the evangelist's office.   But Mr. Ward, high as his name deservedly stands, is not the only one revered in the Christian church, who has held such a sentiment.   Mr. Scott, the commentator, has expressed ideas very similar to the above, as is evident from a quotation from his valuable commentary on Eph. iv. 11., at page 110 of this work.   Dr. Bloomfield, also, in his notes on the same passage, says, respecting the evangelists, that to assisting the apostles "they added the duty of evangelizing the heathen, the kind of duty, in fact, of missionaries in modern times."   In a note, also, on Rom. x. 17, Dr. B. mentions further, "It is remark_ed by Koppe and Rosenmüller, that this passage is simi_lar to verses 14 and 19, and is meant to inculcate the necessity of the evangelical office."   Dr. Winter, also, in a sermon on Eph. iv. 11, supports the same views ; and the late distinguished Robert Hall appears, from some expressions cited at page 88, to have held a simi_lar opinion.   The precise form of the evangelist's office, as continued, is not referred to by these parties ; but that they lean to the idea of its continuance, seems very apparent.

---

* Farewell Letters, p. 20.

The individual, however, who has, so far as the writer knows, most deeply considered this subject, is Mr. Macleod, in his work on Inspiration, frequently referred to in the following pages. In that work, he devotes a whole chapter to the consideration of this office ; and is decided in his views of its permanence, and, also, of its utility in converting the world, and cementing the Christian church. The writer of this work had taken the same view of the subject, and had actually begun to write upon it, before he was aware of Mr. Macleod's opinion. When he met with his volume, he was, however, greatly encouraged ; and he frankly acknowledges himself greatly assisted by it, especially in his views on the spiritual gifts, — a subject the writer conceives of the highest inportance ; as, without an accurate conception of it, confusion is apt to connect itself with all our ideas, not only of the primitive offices and worship, but of the offices and worship, that were designed to be permanent in the church, in all ages. In the following pages, a condensed view is given of this important matter ; and, it is hoped, it may be useful to those into whose hands works of a more elaborate description may not happen to fall.

As to the general execution of the work, the writer regrets not only his inability, but his want of time, and the means of study, to do it all the justice he could have wished. He has, however, done what he could ; and his chief hope in doing so is, that, probably, the work itself, imperfect as it is, may fall into the hands of some one, who, with kindred views and feelings to himself, may, with higher capabilities, present the subject to the Christian public, in a manner much more deeply interesting and impressive. In the mean time, he solicits a careful and candid perusal, by the reader ; and entreats him, neither hastily to receive, nor hastily to condemn what he has written, but patiently to compare it with the oracles of truth. Whatever is in unison with these, however unpopular it may be at present, let him receive ; as, sooner or later, it must prevail : and whatever is not in accordance with these, let him reject ; as, however much it may be cherished now, it will, ultimately, perish before the march of immortal truth, in connexion with that sacred and copious influence that will banish error, during our Redeemer's reign, from this portion of the dominions of God.

Hamsterley, near Bishop Auckland,
December, 1837.

CONTENTS.

ESSAY,

&c. &c.

PART FIRST.

THE NATURE OF THE OFFICE OF THE PRIMITIVE EVANGELIST.

THAT such an office as that of evangelist, was instituted in the Christian church, is clear from the enumeration of the different offices, as stated by the apostle, [*] " He gave some, apostles; and some, prophets; and some, EVANGELISTS; and some, pastors and teachers."—— The office is also said to have been held by Philip, as we find him called an *evangelist*.[†]   Timothy also is called upon to do the *work* of an *evangelist*, [‡]   and, consequently, he must have sustained the office of one.—— As such an office, then, was evidently instituted by our Lord, and held by his disciples, in the primitive age, it may be necessary, in reviewing it, briefly to glance at its *nature*, previously to our presenting any reasons for its *perpetuity*; and in doing so, we shall, as briefly as possible, advert to the following particulars, namely, the character of the evangelists' work ; —— their qualifications, in order to their sustaining that office ; —— their call, and

---

[*] Eph. iv. 11.   [†] Acts xxi. 8.   [‡] 2 Tim. iv. 5.

designation to its exercise;——their authority in the churches;——and the extent of their usefulness, in the church and in the world.

SECTION FIRST.

The character of their work.

Now, as to this, it evidently appears on the face of it, to have been missionary work, and its two distinguishing features are the following, namely, preaching the gospel as itinerants, and planting and watering Christian churches.

Their name plainly points out what they were. Evangelist (ευαγγελιστης) is a Greek term, and its plain meaning, in English, is —— preacher of the gospel. In the original of the New Testament, preaching of the gospel is also called evangelizing (ευαγγελιζομενος).—— Those who evangelised are, however, generally represented as going from place to place, in so doing.—— They were itinerant, not local, or stated, labourers.—— They were, usually, the companions of the apostles, in carrying the commission of Christ into effect, with regard to preaching the gospel to every creature. Such was the case with Timothy and others. Philip, also, was an itinerant. On the persecution that arose about Stephen, he went, we are told, to Samaria, and preached the gospel there, with great success. —— And after instructing, in a more private manner, the Ethiopian Eunuch, being found at Azotus, when he parted from him, he preached, travelling northward, in all the cities and villages, on the coast of the Levant, till he came to Cæsarea. * —— The evangelists. then, evidently, were itinerant preachers.—— As itinerant preachers, however, their labours seem to have had re-

---

1 Acts viii. 4, 40.

spect to two distinct objects, namely, *home*, and *foreign*, exertion. Some of them were home missionaries. Peter is said to be " the apostle of the circumcision." * Hence we find him, generally, labouring among the Jews. He was called, indeed, to open the door of faith to the Gentiles, in the case of Cornelius; but from the phrase used respecting him by Paul, " that the ministry of the circumcision was committed to him," it seems likely that his labours would, chiefly, be confined to Jews, and principally exercised in the Holy Land. He might, indeed, have gone to other places, but in the early, and perhaps, the chief portion, of his missionary career, this seems to have been the principal scene of his labours. Such would be the case, also, with those evangelists, or ministers, that attached themselves to him. Philip may also be termed a home missionary, as his labours do not seem to have extended beyond the limits of Palestine; and, perhaps, generally, in the city of Cæsarea and its vicinity. The whole of the apostles, during the ministry of our Lord, were home missionaries, and so were the seventy, their assistants, who may be regarded as the original evangelists. Our Lord himself was also a home missionary, during his condescending sojourn on earth; and they who are so employed, may, therefore, regard themselves as in good company, and as holding an office peculiarly distinguished.

But amongst the evangelists we find not only home, but *foreign* missionaries. — Paul was so. He was the apostle of the Gentiles; and the ministry of the *uncircumcision* was committed to him, as the ministry of the circumcision was committed to Peter. All his assistants, consequently, would be foreign missionaries, likewise. — Such was Barnabas, Silas, Timothy, Luke, &c.

Whether, however, they acted in the character of home, or of foreign, missionaries, they appear to have had

---

* Gal. ii. 8.

their different districts assigned them.   Paul seems to refer to this, when he says, " *We will not boast of things beyond our* MEASURE, *but according to the* MEASURE of the RULE which GOD hath DISTRIBUTED *to us,* A MEASURE *to* REACH even unto YOU.   *For we* STRETCH *not ourselves* BEYOND *our* MEASURE, *as though we reached not unto you ; for we are come as far as to you also in preaching the gospel of Christ.   Not boasting of things* WITHOUT *our measure, that is,* OF OTHER MEN'S LABOURS ; *but having hope, when your faith is increased, that we shall be enlarged by you* ACCORDING *to* OUR RULE *abundantly, to preach the gospel in the regions beyond you, and not to boast, in* ANOTHER MAN'S LINE, *of things made ready to our hand.* *   The " measure" and "rule," of the apostle, mentioned here, evidently refer to the district of country assigned him to labour in.   Of this we have an instance, when Asia Minor was allotted to him and Barnabas, at the time that the church at Antioch, by command of the Holy Ghost, was called to separate them for the work, whereunto He had assigned them.† The line of another man, also alluded to, seems to imply the same in relation to other labourers, and the general conclusion is, that *each missionary* had his field of labour marked out for him, by the churches, under the immediate direction of the Holy Ghost, speaking, in all likelihood, through the medium of some of the prophets in these churches.   These districts would, probably, be extensive, in the first instance, but as is the case in modern times, in proportion to the increase of missionaries, in like proportion, would their respective boundaries be contracted.

The *home* missionaries would, in all probability, also have their *circuits.*   The apostles, and the seventy, before our Lord's ascension, had their respective districts assigned them.   " *He sent them out two and two, into*

---

* 2 Cor. x. 13-16.   † Acts xiii. 2, 3.

every city and place, whither he himself would come." *
It is not a likely circumstance, that they would all go to
the *same places*; but, in order to save labour, the *whole
country* seems to have been *parcelled out* among them.
One pair would go to one district, and another to another:
the whole country thus becoming the scene of their
united exertions. This practice, in all likelihood, would
be a guide to those evangelists who, afterwards, became,
what may be termed, home, or native missionaries, in a
particular country. The mission of Philip, for instance,
in the Holy Land, would, in all likelihood, be carried on
in a similar manner.

But it may be noticed, finally, with regard to the line
of operation, or district of labour, of these missionaries,
that, generally speaking, they would be *moveable* from
one district to another. Paul frequently changed his
district: sometimes, he laboured in Syria, at other times,
in Cilicia, at other times in Pamphylia, and other pro-
vinces in Asia Minor. Then we find him in Macedonia;
afterward in Achaia; then in Illyiricum; and then at
Rome. His assistants, also, the evangelists, sometimes went with him in these rounds; and, at other
times, *he* went to one district, and *they* to another.
Timotheus and Erastus were sent into Macedonia, when
Paul was at Ephesus. At another time Timothy was
left at Ephesus, when Paul went to Macedonia. At one
time, also, we find Titus labouring in Crete; and at another, in Dalmatia. At one time, also, Tychicus was sent
to Collosse; and, at another, either he, or Artemas, was
sent to succeed Titus, in his labours, in Crete. Philip
also, in all likelihood, did not remain always in Cæsarea,
though he is represented as having a house there. He
does not appear to have been there, when Cornelius was
directed to send to Joppa for Peter. — Peter was itinerating on the sea coast, at that time, and Philip might be

---

* Matt. x. 5. Luke x. 1
B 3

in the interior, probably revisiting the church in Samaria, that he had been the means of planting. *   The
twelve apostles, and the seventy also, as home missionaries, supposing them to have gone out more than once,
would, likely, be sent out by our Lord, on the same principle—the district of each pair would, likely, be changed.
In all these points, then, the original missionaries may be
regarded as patterns to missionary labourers, home and
foreign, of modern times.

The second great leading feature in the work of an
evangelist was, the planting and watering of Christian
churches. —

In the first place, they planted churches; and this
they did, in the first instance, by separating the newly
converted from the world.   Paul is represented as acting on this principle at Ephesus; hence it is said, that,
" when divers," to whom he spake, " were hardened, and
believed not, but spake evil of that way before the multitude, Paul departed from them, and separated the disciples, disputing daily in the school of one Tyrannus." †
The disciples, then, instead of going to the Jewish syna-
gogue, to worship, assembled in a school-room, and were
there formed into a Christian society, or church, Εκκλησια,
a called out, a select, or separated band of believing men.
This is what Paul did as a missionary, to those to whom
he had been rendered useful: all missionaries would,
doubtless, act on the same principle.   But they not only
formed them into select bodies, but they guided them in
the selection of office-bearers, and presided at their ordination.

They guided them, in the first place, in the selection
of their office-bearers; and they did so, by pointing out the
two kinds of officers needful for them, namely, bishops,

---

* It cannot be affirmed, that Peter was sent to confer the gifts
of the Holy Spirit, as the Holy Ghost is represented as falling on
the household of Cornelius, without the laying on of his hands.
Acts x. 44, &c.   † Acts xix. 9.

or superintendants, and deacons, or assistants. [*] The first were to episcopize, namely, oversee, or superintend the spiritual state of the body; and they were to do so by presiding over them; taking the lead in worship and the administration of ordinances; by instructing them in the knowledge of the scriptures, publicly and privately; by visiting them, to see that they walked orderly; to correct them when they did wrong; and to excommunicate them when they were incorrigible. The deacons were to deaconize, namely, serve the church, and assist the bishops in a variety of ways; by providing for the poor, and for the support of the gospel; by visiting the sick, and by teaching, according to their ability. This class appears to have been selected from both sexes; hence Phebe is said to have been a servant, or deaconess of the church of Cenchrea; [†] and the widows referred to in 1 Tim. v. 9, are supposed to have been of the same class. The qualifications of each kind of officers, are distinctly stated in 1 Tim. iii. 1-13. Those who were called to sustain the offices, were required, in the first instance, to be proved, by comparing their natural capacity, and their moral character, with the qualification required in each; and those only who possessed these qualifications, were to be eligible.

It has been supposed, by some, that the apostles, or evangelists alone, had the choice and ordination of these officers. This, however, seems to be a mistake. By comparing one part of the New Testament with another, we shall be led to perceive, that the churches had, in this matter, as important a duty to fulfil as the evangelists. The one party had to choose, and the other to ordain, or appoint. This was the case, beyond the shadow of a doubt, with one class of officers, namely, the deacons, as we perceive in the instance of the deacons of the church in Jerusalem. The qualifications of these

---

[*] 1 Tim. iii. 1-13, and Titus i. 5-9.   [†] Rom. xvi. 1.

were stated, by the apostles, to the multitude of the disciples in that church, and they — the multitude — were
called to *"look out from among themselves,"* a suitable
number of men, "whom they"—the apostles—"might
appoint, or ordain over this business." All this was
done, — the disciples chose them, and the apostles ordained them, by the laying on of their hands. *

Such was the way the deacons were chosen, at Jerusalem; and we have no reason to believe that they would
be chosen differently, in other churches. The deacons,
then, that Timothy was called upon to lay his hands on,
were, doubtless, chosen in the same way; so would the
deacons of the churches in Crete, that Titus ordained;
and so also the deacons, in the churches in Asia Minor,
that Paul and Barnabas ordained. It is not at all probable that, in any case, it would be otherwise. It is not to
be supposed that an apostle, in his individual capacity,
would do that, which was not done by the apostles, as an
aggregate body. And if so with an *apostle,* far less with
an *evangelist.* This is confirmed, by the character of the
choice of the messengers selected by the churches, to carry their bounty to the poor saints at Jerusalem. Of one of
these it is said, that he was " chosen (χειροτονηθεις) of the
churches." The original term implies election by a shew
of hands. † Now this happened in the churches of
Macedonia, and had a relation to a delegate, whose duty
greatly resembled that of a deacon. The popular choice,
then, in both cases, seems to intimate, that the mode of
selection, in the case of deacons, was alike in all the
churches, however remotely situated from one another.
Nor is there any ground, from any quarter, to conclude,
that the choice of the bishops, was, in any way, different
from that of the deacons. No difference is hinted at in
the directions given to Timothy. He is called upon to lay
hands on both classes equally, after they had been proved

---

* Acts vi. 2-6.   † 2 Cor. viii. 19.

to possess certain qualifications; and as the churches were called to judge of these qualifications, in the case of their electing deacons, so, as there is no hint to the contrary, it is probable, — highly probable indeed, that the people equally judged of the qualifications of the bishops. This is confirmed by the conduct of the apostles, in the case of Matthias, he being chosen to the apostolate.* They acted on the same principle that they did afterward, in the case of deacons. They referred the election to the multitude of the disciples, *as far as they could carry it in such a case.* The usage of the church in the second century, is also confirmatory of this idea. The people at large then chose their bishop. † It seems also hinted at in what Paul enjoins on Timothy. "Lay hands suddenly on no man, neither be a partaker of other men's sins: keep thyself pure." ‡ This admonition seems to imply the following things. In the first place, that other men had to do in the selection of those on whom hands were to be laid, as well as Timothy. — Secondly, that these other men might sin, in the part they took, in the selection. They might act on the principle of partiality, to certain individuals, instead of being guided by the directions given them respecting the qualifications of bishops, and thereby put improper persons into the office. Thirdly, Timothy is enjoined to oppose this kind of election, by not concurring in it. "Do nothing by partiality. Lay hands suddenly on no man." Fourthly, he is not to be guided merely by the election of any church, and to ordain none except he is acquainted with

---

* Acts i. 15-26.

† Eusebius, in his Ecclesiastical History, Book vi. chap. 28, affirms that the brethren were gathered together for the election of a bishop, after the death of Anterus, bishop of Rome ; and that the whole multitude, moved, as they conceived, by a particular signal, cried out cheerfully with one accord, that Fabianus was worthy of the bishoprick ; and he was, accordingly, taken and installed bishop.

‡ 1 Tim. v. 22.

him, and is persuaded that he has the qualifications required for the office.—— Fifthly, this applies to both classes of officers — as qualification is required in the case of both, and hands are to be laid on both. All these circumstances, then, united, seem to prove, that the mode of selection, and ordination to both offices, was the same. The people elected, and the missionaries, when they were satisfied, respecting the propriety of the choice, ordained. The following terms, then, seems to have all one meaning, namely, "whom we may appoint," Κατασησωμεν. Acts vi. 3; and, " ordain, (Καταστησην.) elders, in every city." Titus i. 5; and " ordained, (Χειροτησαντες) them elders in every church, Acts xiv. 23; and lay hands (Χειρας-επιτιθει) suddenly on no man," 1 Tim. v. 22. All these terms refer to the appointments to office, by the apostles, or evangelists, after the selection of the people. This, then, we trust, clearly shows the part the evangelists had, in setting in order the things that were wanting in the churches, by ordaining elders, in every city. Their duty was none other than what may be equally well discharged, by any modern missionary. They guided the newly formed churches, in the choice of their office-bearers, and than presided at their ordination.

But the primitive missionaries *watered* the churches as well as planted them. The planting, however, was sometimes performed by one party, and the watering by another, "I have planted," says Paul, "and Apollos watered." * Sometimes, both duties were performed, by the same individual, or individuals. Paul and Barnabas, not only gathered the churches in Asia Minor, but they revisited them. They did so, in order to confirm them in the faith and purity of the gospel; hence they are said, to have confirmed the souls of the disciples; exhorting them to continue in the faith," &c. † They watered the churches, however, not only by revisiting them, but

---

* 1 Cor. iii. 6.   † Acts xiv. 21, 22.

also by leaving one of their number behind them, far_ther to instruct the disciples, and to oppose any heresies, that might creep in among them. Such was the manner in which Paul watered the church at Ephesus. "I besought thee," says he to Timothy, "to abide still at Ephesus, that thou mightest charge some that they teach no other doctrine." * Again, "if thou put the brethren in remembrance of these things, thou shalt be a good minister of Jesus Christ." It was to water the churches in Crete, that Titus was sent there, to set in order the things that were wanting; and for the same object, were other evangelists sent to visit other churches. It is natural for a parent to feel for his children. It is natural for him to fear lest disease should overtake them. It is natural for him to have them fed with wholesome food, that they may become strong, healthy, and vigorous. It is so with a spiritual father, as well as a natural one. Paul, that great pattern to all missionaries, felt thus towards his spiritual children,—— those whom he had been the means of converting; and the care he had for them, was like a heavy weight upon his shoulders; hence, after enumerating his various troubles as a Christian minister, he sums up the whole, by saying, "besides those things that are without, that which cometh on me daily, the care of all the churches." † This care is most admirably referred to, in the manner in which he addresses the church at Philippi, with respect to Timothy, who was about to visit them, in order to know their spiritual condition. "But I trust in the Lord Jesus to send Timotheus shortly unto you, that I also may be of good comfort, when I know your state; for I have no man likeminded, who will naturally care for your state; for all seek their own, not the things which are Jesus Christ's. But ye know the proof of him, that as a son with the father, he hath served with me in the gospel." ‡ Such

---

* Tim. i. 3, and iv. 6. † 2 Cor. xi. 28. ‡ Phil. ii. 19-22.

was the care of the first missionaries, for all the different
churches they had been the means of gathering.   They
visited them as often as they could, personally, and when
that could not be accomplished, they wrote letters to
them, by the hands of messengers, who, being fellow labourers, felt nearly as deep an interest in the spiritual
well-being of the parties concerned, as themselves.   See
2 Cor. vii. 4-16, and 1 Thess. iii. 1-13.

SECTION SECOND.

The gifts, or qualifications, of the primitive evangelists.

These may be divided into two classes, namely, ordinary, and extraordinary.   The ordinary were those necessary to be possessed by all Christian ministers, in every
age ; the extraordinary were adapted to the exigencies of
the Christian religion, during the apostolic age.   The
first, are enumerated in the epistles of Paul to the evangelists Timothy and Titus, and the other, in the twelfth
chapter of the first epistle to the Corinthians.   The
moral virtues, and Christian graces, included in the first,
are so clearly perceptible, that they require but little
notice.   The latter, however, require some further consideration, in order to our being better able to decide on
the question,—Whether the office of evangelist was a
temporary or a permanent one ?

The gifts of the primitive church, seem to have been
divided into three distinct classes, namely, first, those
which relate to religious thought, or idea.   Second,
those which relate to the communication of such
thought ; and, third, those that refer to its confirmation.

The endowments, which relate to the possession of
religious idea, or thought, were, the WORD of WISDOM,—
the GIFT of PROPHECY, and the WORD of KNOWLEDGE ;
those that relate to the communication of thought, were,
the gift of tongues, and the interpretation of tongues ;

and those which regarded the confirmation of the ideas, exhibited as the truth of God were, the gifts of healing, and other miraculous powers. The first three, were possessed, severally, by the three different kinds of instructors, who, at that early period of the church, were called, either to convert the world, or to build up believers on their most holy faith. The other two, seem to have been possessed, in common, by each of these three classes of instructors; though, it is probable, they were possessed, in a higher degree, by some, than by others. Such, then, were the principal endowments: there were, however, two others, that seem, likewise in a great degree, common to all — not only to instructors, but the instructed. These were *faith*, and the *discerning* of *spirits*. As to the first of these, it seems to have been that firm confidence in God, which led its possessors to brave danger,* and also enabled them to work miracles.† It was necessary, then, to all who had, for the sake of the Redeemer, dangers to overcome; and also, to all those who proved the Christian doctrines, by their miraculous doings. As to the discerning of spirits, this was a duty enjoined on all Christians. They were called upon " not to believe every spirit, but to try the spirits whether they were of God."‡ There were some, however, who, in all likelihood, possessed this endowment in a much higher degree than others. These were they, who, in 1 Cor. xiv. 29, are called upon to judge, — " Let the prophets speak two or three, and let the other judge." Some suppose these latter were they that, are termed " governments" or directors; while the interpreters of tongues, are supposed to have been those called " helps." ‖

---

* Heb. xi. 23-38.   † Luke xvii. 5, 6, & 1 Cor. xiii. 2.
‡ John iv. 1.
‖ Both of these endowments would be of essential use at that period; the first to ascertain the reality of the inspiration of those who pretended to it — for this is the discernment spoken of, and

C.

It is, however, to the three classes of instructors, and their three peculiar gifts for instruction, that our attention is particularly called.—— As to the three classes of instructors, Paul refers to them, in the following terms, "God hath set some in the church, first apostles, secondarily prophets, thirdly teachers. Now to each of these, respectively, the three above endowments seem to have belonged ; the word of wisdom, to the apostles; the gift of prophecy, to the prophets ; and the word of knowledge, to the teachers.—We shall take a brief glance at each of these classes of instructors, and their respective endowments.

With regard to the first,—the apostles—their endowment, the *word of wisdom*, seems to have been equivalent to that of REVELATION. Hence Paul represents himself, and his fellow apostles, as speaking the WISDOM of God, — that wisdom, he adds, was previously " a mystery," namely, hidden, or concealed, from the wise men and the princes of this world, but he further adds, " God hath REVEALED them — i. e. the things prepared for them that love him — unto us by his Spirit." *
The wisdom of God, or word of wisdom, then, includes the revelation of the various doctrines, and duties, and institutions of Christianity, which the apostles, as God's immediate ambassadors, taught the sons of men. The epistle to the Romans is, perhaps, the brightest specimen of the possession of this gift, that we have on record. —— As to the prophets, there can be little doubt that the gift of prophecy attached to them. †   This en-

---

not the moral characters of individuals ; the second, was needful not only to interpret what was spoken, in the churches, in strange languages — but also, in the translation of the Hebrew scriptures into Greek, or any other language. The gospel of Matthew is said to have been written originally in Hebrew ; if so, it is highly probable that our present Greek copy was translated, either by himself, or by some one under his direction, or by one of these *Helps.*

* 1 Cor. ii. 6-10.

† Drs. Benson and Macknight suppose, that the enumeration

dowment may be regarded as the best known of the three, as it has been possessed by many individuals under the former, as well as under the present, dispensation. Under both dispensations, the prophetic functions were nearly similar. These appear to have been the three following—foretelling future events — instruct-

---

of the *gifts*, by the apostle, in 1 Cor. xii. 8-10, corresponds, in point of *order*, with the enumeration of *offices* in the 28th and 29th verses of the same chapter ; and, consequently, they apply the word of knowledge to the prophets. The prophets, they also divide into two classes, the superior, and inferior ; and to these latter they apply the gift of prophecy, stated after, and the word of knowledge, to the former. This distinction, however, among the prophets, is one nowhere hinted at in scripture ; and besides, as the *order* of the enumeration is not *equal*, in *other respects*, as in the case of *healings* and *miracles*, it seems most natural to classify the gifts with the offices to which they appear naturally to belong. It is most natural to assign the gift of prophecy, to the prophets ; and this seems adapted, as a clue, to guide us in our application of the others. Such is the view taken by Mr. Macleod in his excellent work intitled, "A view of Inspiration, comprehending the nature and distinctions of the spiritual gifts and offices of the apostolic age." — A work, the writer would strongly recommend, to all who wish to understand those parts of the New Testament which relate to the somewhat difficult subject of spiritual gifts.

The following is a tabular view of the classification of the spiritual gifts and offices, in the three different lists given by the apostle, in the 12th chap. of 1 Cor., by each of the above parties : —

DRS. BENSON and MACKNIGHT, &c.'s view.

1st List.	2nd List.	3rd List.
The word of wisdom.	Apostles.	Apostles.
The word of knowledge.	Prophets.	Prophets.
Faith.	Teachers.	Teachers.
Miracles.	Miracles.	Miracles.
Healing.	Healing.	Healing.
Prophecy.	Helps.	} Tongues.
Discernment of spirits.	Governments.	
Tongues.	Tongues.	
Interpretations. }	Tongues.	Interpreters.
Tongues.		

ing the people — and leading the praises of God, in worshipping assemblies. The first of these is, however, the distinguishing characteristic of a prophet. This is, indeed, the idea we, generally, and principally, attach to the office ; and prophesying, we, usually, understand to be foretelling events yet to come. Such were the pro. phecies of David, Isaiah, Daniel, and others, respecting the Messiah, and the different kingdoms of the world. Such were those of Agabus, who prophesied of the dearth, in the days of Claudius, and also respecting the imprisonment of Paul. Such, also, were those of Paul, who prophesied of the man of sin ; and such were the prophecies of John, who, in the book of Revelation, un-folded the history of the church, till the end of time.

But the communication of instruction, on the subject of religion, was also another important function attending prophesying. This duty seems to have been nearly equivalent to preaching in modern times ; with the exception of its being under an inspired impulse, or revelation. From the days of Samuel, at least, there seems to have been a race of individuals raised up, in almost constant succession, whose business seems to have been, to teach the people in the knowledge of the divine writings, and to warn them of their sins. The writings of Jeremiah, Ezekiel, Hosea, and others of the prophets, in many places, illustrate this part of the

---

MR. MACLEOD's view.

1st List.	2nd List.	3rd List.
The word of wisdom.	Apostles.	Apostles.
Prophecy.	Prophets.	Prophets.
The word of knowledge.	Teachers.	Teachers.
Tongues.	Tongues.	Tongues.
Interpretations.	Helps.	Interpreters.
Discerning of spirits.	Governments.	————
Miracles.	Miracles.	Miracles.
Healings.	Healings.	Healings.
Faith.		

subject. John the Baptist, who is said to have been taken by the people for a prophet, and of whom, our Lord himself affirms, that a greater prophet had not arisen, was a prophet of this description. Of a like class, were the prophets that spake to *edification*, to *exhortation*, and *comfort*, in the first Christian churches.* The hortatory parts of the epistles, may be regarded as specimens of this kind of prophesying.

In addition, prophesying included the performance the praise of God, in public or private worship. Both males and females seem to have engaged, as prophets and prophetesses, in this delightful exercise. Asaph, Heman, Jeduthun, with their twenty-four sons, are said to prophecy in leading the praise of the Tabernacle.† On this account, also, is Miriam, the sister of Moses, called a prophetess;‡ and it is highly probable, that the four daughters of Philip, are said to prophecy, from their performance of this same duty.‖

There was a peculiarity about the inspiration of the prophets. It came upon them, with a sudden impetus. Some of those, inspired prophetically under the old dispensation, seem to have felt in this way. The most striking instances of this kind, are, perhaps, the cases of Balaam and of Saul. Of the first, it is said, "The spirit of the Lord came upon him, and the man whose eye had been shut but was now open, said, how goodly are thy tents, O Jacob," &c. § Of the latter, it is said, "the spirit of the Lord came on him, and he stripped off his clothes and prophesied."¶ The prophets in the church at Corinth, are also spoken of, as having something revealed to them, in such a way, as was difficult for them

---

* That these spoke by immediate inspiration, appears evident from what the apostle says, 1 Cor. xiv. 30, "If anything be *revealed* to another that sitteth by, let the first hold his peace."

† 1 Chron. xxv. 1-3. ‡ Exodus xv. 20-21. ‖ Acts xxi. 9.

§ Num. xxiv. 3-5. ¶ 1 Sam xix 22-24.

to restrain themselves. "If any thing be revealed to another that sitteth by, let the first hold his peace, for, ye may all prophesy, one by one, that all may learn, and all may be comforted; and the spirits of the prophets are subject to the prophets; for God is not the author of confusion, but of peace, as in all the churches of the saints."*

In relation to the third class of instructors, and their gifts, we have already noticed that they were called *teachers*, and their endowment was the *word* of *knowledge*. The teachers spoken of, by the apostle, in the end of the twelfth chapter of his first epistle to the Corinthians, seem to have included all the other instructors in the church, besides the apostles and the prophets. These other are referred to, in the enumeration of offices, by Paul, in Eph. iv. 11, as evangelists, pastors, and teachers. All these, then, seem to have been included in the *general* term,—— *teachers,* in the other passage. All of them, indeed, elsewhere, appear to be called teachers; hence the teachers at Antioch, spoken of in Acts xiii. 1, were, probably, those evangelists that left Jerusalem, at the same time that Philip did, and went every where preaching the word; and some of them, it is said, travelled as far as Phenice, and Cyprus, and Antioch, preaching the word to none but Jews only. They are termed teachers, to distinguish them from the prophets, who are also said to be there. The pastors, also, as teachers, seem referred to when the apostle says, Rom. xii. 7, "or he that teacheth, on teaching."—— It is highly probable, then, that all these are included in this term. All of them, we know, *were endowed.* Personally, indeed, they might be said to be bestowed as gifts on men; but this was, by themselves being gifted. The evangelists, the pastors, and teachers, were, therefore, all endowed men, as well as the apostles and pro-

---

* 1 Cor. xiv. 30-33.

phets. The question, then, is, In what did the endowment of the three former, as teachers, consist ? It was
not the word of wisdom, for that belonged to the apostles. It was not the gift of prophecy, or they must
have been prophets. There was, then, only one other
gift remaining, namely, the word of knowledge : it seems
reasonable, therefore, to suppose, that this endowment
was theirs. It belonged to one and all of them. The
pastor, then, and the evangelist, as teachers, were on
the same footing, in point of endowment. As teachers,
in all probability, they possessed the endowment, originally, and afterwards, were selected, each to his separate
department of labour; the evangelist to convert the
world; and the pastor to edify believers. The teachers,
also, mentioned in Eph. iv. 11, were, probably, those
who, in the churches, either as deacons, or, unofficially,
used the gift for the edification of their brethren.

But what was the character of the endowment itself?
It is nowhere defined in the New Testament. The
name, however, seems to suggest the *idea* of what it was.
This is the case with the word of wisdom. It is,
also, nowhere defined ; yet its name seems, naturally,
to suggest what was its character. So with the word
of knowledge. We know the common relation subsisting between wisdom and knowledge. Wisdom suggests
the idea of original genius ; and knowledge that of bare
information. The one reflects the other, as the moon,
and other luminaries, reflect the rays of the sun. It is
so, in the case alluded to. The wisdom of God, spoken
by the apostles, came from them as original matter. The
word of knowledge, was only the reflection of this, as
coming from the evangelists and pastors. It seems to
have included two things, namely, a *clear understanding*
and a *ready recollection* of what the apostles made
known, as the *revelation* of the divine mind, as well as
a distinct understanding of the Old Testament scriptures.
The first of these, appears to be referred to in the declaration, — "Then opened he their understandings

that they might understand the scripture ;" * the second, also, in those expressions of our Lord to his disciples,— " But the comforter who is the Holy Ghost,—he shall teach you all things, and bring all things to your remembrance, whatsoever I have said unto you."—† Now, such a gift was especially needed at that time, on two accounts — first, on account of the absence of the complete canon of scripture ; and, secondly, on account of the numbers of gifted individuals that were then in the several churches. ‡

When we look, also, at what is said, in connexion with the gift of Timothy, we shall find additional evidence, that this gift was the one which belonged to the evangelists. Although this gift, is said to have been bestowed by prophecy it was nevertheless not prophecy *itself.* This is evident from the apostle calling on Timothy, "to stir it up," and " not to neglect it."— The prophets, as we have seen, had rather to *restrain,* than to *stir up,* their gift. Timothy, however, was called on, to "stir up" his. Besides, this gift seems to have been capable of improvement, by reading, — "Till I come, give attendance to reading, to exhortation, to doctrine."— ‖ The fair inference, then, seems to be, that the gift itself had a reference to knowledge ; and what that knowledge was, appears afterwards to be stated, as " *the form or outline* — *υποτυπωσιν* — *of sound words,*

---

* Luke xxiv. 45.   † John xiv. 26.

‡ There seems no proper ground for believing that any one taught in the primitive church, without spiritual gifts. As these gifts abounded in the churches, and were actually given for instruction, so it would have been preposterous in any, to have attempted to teach without them. The case of Apollos is not in point, as he was precisely in the condition of the twelve men at Ephesus, who knew only the baptism of John, when he preached in the Jewish Synagogues. Like them, also, he would, doubtless, receive the gifts of the Holy Ghost.

‖ 1 Tim. iv. 13-14, and 2 Tim. i. 6.

which he (Timothy) had heard of the apostle " " That good thing," also, says the apostle to him, " committed to thee," or deposited with thee, "*keep*," or *guard*, "through the Holy Ghost, that dwelleth in us."[*] What this *good thing* was, seems to be still more clearly exhibited, by being put in *contrast* with its *opposite*, in another passage. " O Timothy ; keep that which is committed to thy trust, avoiding profane and vain babblings, and oppositions of *science*, or knowledge, (γνωσις) falsely so called, which some professing, have erred concerning the faith."[†] The knowledge here spoken of, was, doubtless, what Paul elsewhere calls " *the form of knowledge, and of the truth in the law*," of which the speculative Jew made his boast.[‡] —— It seems, then, but reasonable to conclude, that Timothy's gift was " the word of knowledge."

But the same may be affirmed of the other evangelists, so far as we are able to trace. Such appears to have been the gift of Stephen, from the view we find him taking of the Jewish history in the seventh of the Acts. Of Philip, also, in his explanation of the fifty-third of Isaiah, to the Ethiopian Eunuch. It appears to have been the gift, likewise, by which Luke wrote his gospel, and the Acts of the Apostles, and by which Mark wrote the gospel that goes by his name. Neither of these evangelists was an eye witness of the facts he states ; but Luke is supposed to have written under the guidance of Paul ; and also, as he himself tells us, of those who had been, from the beginning, " eye witnesses and ministers of the Word.'[||] Mark, by the general consent of antiquity, is said to have written his gospel under the immediate inspection of the apostle Peter.[§] The epistle

---

[*] 2 Tim. i. 13-14. [†] 1 Tim. vi. 20. [‡] Rom. ii. 20. [||] Luke i. 1-4.

[§] The four biographers of our Lord are usually termed evangelists, and this title was very ancient, as we find them so called by Eusebius. This title, however, is never given them in the scriptures.

to the Hebrews. however, is, perhaps, the most perfect specimen of the word of knowledge that we possess, in the sacred record.

That the pastors, also, possessed this gift, seems intimated, from the similarity of the language addressed to them, to that addressed to Timothy. Hence Titus is called on to give them in charge, to " hold fast the faithful word as they have been taught, that they may be able, by sound doctrine, both to exhort and to convince the gainsayers." *

Such, then, is the word of knowledge — so far as we can judge in the case. As an endowment, it was inferior to both the word of wisdom and the gift of prophecy; but still, it answered well the purposes for which it was given. By the use of the *superior gifts,* the *apostles* and *prophets* laid the *foundation* of the Christian church. The one, as the first missionaries to the world, and the other, as the first instructors in the churches. Hence says Paul, respecting the church in general, " *And are built upon the foundation of the apostles and prophets, Jesus Christ himself being the chief corner stone.*† The evangelists, and pastors, and teachers, first assisted, and then succeeded these; and, by the use of the word of knowledge, successfully reared the fabric, during the first century; and thus, by what may be termed their *intermediate endowment,* gradually prepared the way for the labours of those, from whom extraordinary gifts were altogether withdrawn; and who were left to carry on the same cause, under ordinary circumstances, namely, the complete Christian canon — the ordinary influence of the Holy Spirit — and the modicum of natural talent with which they were furnished. ‡

---

* Titus i. 9.   † Eph. ii. 20.

‡ That the gifts of the first age were to cease, is plainly intimated, by the apostle, 1 Cor. xiii. 8. The cause of this ceasing is *not* spoken of as arising from the apostacy of Christians, but

SECTION THIRD.

The nature of the call of the evangelists, and their designation.

The *appointment* of this office, like all the others, was made by our Lord himself. He gave some, to be evangelists, as well as others, to be apostles, prophets, pastors, and teachers. He appointed the seventy, as assistants to the twelve, during his personal ministry;

---

rather from the perfection of Revelation, which would, ere long, be enjoyed by the church, when the writings of the apostles would all be collected into one volume, for its future edification, and its final appeal, in case of any controversy. Compare 1 Cor. xiii. 9, 10, and Eph. iv. 11-16. It is nowhere hinted, that these gifts shall be revived, if once withdrawn. The completion and confirmation of scripture rendered them necessary at the time they were given, but when these ends were answered, they were no longer required. Unless something, then, is necessary to be added to the Bible, and that addition need to be confirmed, we cannot conceive of any further necessity for these endowments. God does not bestow his gifts for mere parade. He has always an important end to serve when he interferes with the ordinary arrangements of nature. Besides, it is plainly intimated in the book of Revelation, chap. xxii. 18, 19, that addition or subtraction from the volume at large, which it terminates, is regarded as one of the greatest of crimes. The pretensions, then, of all who profess to be inspired, extraordinarily, ought ever to be suspected. The scriptures, as a whole, are represented as being adapted to all those matters which tend to make the man of God perfect, and, as such is the case, all that appears necessary for the Christian church, after the completion of the canon of revelation, is, the careful, daily, use of the whole, in combination with the ordinary influence of the Holy Spirit. "Open thou mine eyes," says David, "that I may see wondrous things out of thy law." The scriptures, employed thus, we shall find sufficient for all religious ends. They will make wise unto salvation — convert the soul — and build us up and give us an inheritance among the sanctified.

and, it is highly probable, employed them, as evangelists, after his ascension. It was he, also, who *qualified* the different classes of labourers, for the discharge of their several duties. The bestowment, then, of a *qualification*, for the office of evangelist, as well as for any other office, must be regarded as equivalent to a *call*, to exercise that office. Endowments would not be granted, where they were not intended to be employed. The possession, then, of qualification for the office, would be regarded as an undoubted call to it. This was the case with those who sustained the pastoral office; hence they are required to have certain qualifications, before they exercised it. In addition to the necessary moral qualifications, they must be "apt to teach." When these were proved, then they were called, by their brethren, to the office, and the hands of the evangelist were laid upon them.* In a manner, similar to this, do the evangelists seem to have been called to the exercise of the duties of their office. Hence, of Timothy, it is said, that "he was well reported of, by the brethren that were at Lystra, and Iconium." Like the bishops and deacons, elected by their brethren, to sustain office in the church, Timothy was found by his brethren, to be a man of good report, and they reported him as such, to Paul and Silas. The result was — that being *proved by the brethren*, he was ordained to the evangelists office, by the laying on of the hands of Paul, and the *presbytery*,— the *eldership*, probably of *both* the churches of Lystra and Iconium. Silas, in all likelihood, would preside along with them. Compare Acts xvi. 1-3, with 1 Tim. iv. 14, and 2 Tim. i. 6.

Such appear to be all the ordinary circumstances, attendant on the ordination of an evangelist, at that period. In Timothy's case, however, there seems to

---

* 1 Tim. iii. 1-10 and 22.

have been something peculiar to the times, — there were prophetic intimations given respecting him, it would appear, from what Paul says, 1 Tim. i. 18. His gift is also said to have been "given him by prophecy," intimating, probably, that he had been pointed out, by some of the prophets, in the churches of Lystra and Iconium, as one that would, in future, be a useful man; and, in consequence of this, as well as the good report of the brethren, Paul and the presbytery laid their hands on him. This, however, appears to amount to no more, than what is said of some of the pastors of the same period. Hence the elders of the church at Ephesus are said to have been "made overseers, by the Holy Ghost," * meaning, probably, some prophetic intimation to engage in the work, as in the case of Timothy. This circumstance, therefore, must be regarded as not peculiar to the office of evangelists, but to the times in which they lived. If it were otherwise then, it must have been equally peculiar to the pastoral office. Their call and designation to their office, then, seem, in the case of the evangelists, to be placed on the same footing, with those of the bishops and deacons of the same period. They were proved by the brethren, and ordained by the presbyters, and the presbyters, on the other hand, were proved by the brethren, and ordained by them.

As to the ordination itself, it seems to have proceeded by fasting and prayer, and the laying on of hands. With regard to this latter practice, it seems, evidently, to have been a Jewish custom, and used on different occasions, such as the bestowment of blessings — the confession of sin — and designation to office. It was thus that Jacob blessed the sons of Joseph. † It was by laying his hands on the head of the scape goat, that the priest confessed the sins of the people; ‡ and it was

---

* Acts xx. 28.　　† Gen. xlviii. 14.　　‡ Lev. xvi. 21.

D

by **Moses** laying his hands on him, that Joshua was designated to his office.* The same custom was adopted into the Christian church, and was used in imparting spiritual gifts, and also in ordaining, or appointing, the evangelists, the bishops, and the deacons, to their respective offices. The same practice seems also to have been employed, in connection with prayer, when any of the ministers of that period, were sent on special missions, and also in relation to the sick. † *Prayer*, however, was the *principal* matter on these occasions, and *fasting* was only employed to give *edge* to it. The laying on of hands was, in itself, a mere form, having no particular virtue attached to it. This ought to be carefully marked, lest any superstitious idea should be appended to it. As, however, it prevailed in the apostolic age of the church, there can no harm arise from its use, provided the idea now mentioned, be ever kept in view.

Such is the character of the call and designation of the primitive evangelists. It may, however, be worthy of notice here that, when designated to missionary work, generally speaking, they seem to have been sent out *two* and *two*. ‡ Such was the way in which our Lord himself acted, in sending out the twelve, and the seventy. He knew that man is a social being, and, consequently, greatly improved in all his undertakings by sociality. He, himself, had known the value of social struggles, and he delighted in rewarding the companions of his toils. — "Ye are they," said he to his disciples, "that have continued with me in all my temptations, and I appoint unto you a kingdom, as my Father hath appointed unto me." ‖ This principle seems, pretty generally, acted on afterwards. Hence Peter and John were often together. So also Paul and Barnabas, and Paul and Silas. Timo-

---

* Deut. xxxiv. 9. † 1 Tim. iv. 14, and v. 22; and Acts vi. 6; xiii. 3, and xxviii 8.   ‡ Luke x. 1.   ‖ Luke xxii. 28, 29.

theus and Erastus are also said to have gone together to Macedonia. *   It is true that, at times, we read of only one going on special missions, such as the mission of Timothy to Ephesus, of Titus to Crete, and of Barnabas to Antioch. †   Not unfrequently, however, there were found together, in their missionary peregrinations, more even than two.   Sometimes we find a number, all working in harmony, such as Paul, Silas, Luke, and Timothy.‡ In fine, such seems, in a great degree, the intention of the office of evangelist.   He was the *social friend* — the *companion* — the *minister* — the *assistant* of an apostle ; and, doubtless, when the apostles expired, the evangelists themselves would have similar assistants, in carrying on their missionary labours, throughout the world.

Section Fourth.

On the authority of the evangelists in the churches.

It is generally supposed, and said, that the evangelists had great authority in the churches.   What that authority was, and what its extent, becomes, then, a very interesting question.   We have already seen the amount of their authority, as far as ordination is concerned.   As in the case of the apostles themselves, — the people chose, and they ordained, after they were satisfied that the choice was prudent.   A veto on the selection, and the act of ordination, included all the power they possessed in this matter.   Wherein else, then, lay their power ?   It may be said, — in the authority with which they *rebuked* in preaching.   But what did they rebuke ? Doubtless, sin and error.   With what *authority* did they

---

* Acts iii. 1-14 ; xiii. 2-52 ; xiv. 1-27 ; xv. 40-41, and xix. 22.
† 1 Tim. i. 3 ; Titus i. 5 ; and Acts xi. 22.
‡ Acts xvi. 10, and xvii. 15.

do so?   Not their own, nor even that of an apostle, in himself considered.   It was solely the authority of the truth of God.   Even an apostle had no authority but this.   All the authority that the apostles, as a body, had in the churches, sprung from their possession of the word of wisdom, namely, the revelation they had of the will of God.   Whatever authority, then, the evangelists displayed in reproving, was only the authority of scripture.   Hence Timothy is called " to reprove, rebuke, exhort, in preaching the *word*," because, "all scripture is given by inspiration of God, and is profitable for *reproof*, for *correction*, and for instruction in righteousness, that the man of God may be perfect, thoroughly furnished unto all good works. *   But still, it may be said, an evangelist came directly from those who were entrusted with the communication of the divine will to men.   It is true he did, and it must be confessed, that this carries it in it the appearance of his possessing more than common authority.   It is this, doubtless, that has invested the term authority, as applied to the evangelists, with a kind of charm.   But when the matter is investigated, we shall find that, as far as authority is concerned, there is more of appearance than reality in it.   Like Timothy's call by prophecy, this circumstance belonged more to the age in which they lived, than to the office that they sustained.   It was a merely adventitious circumstance, arising out of the then state of things ; for, supposing the apostles to be dead, and all their writings collected, so that both the evangelists and the churches acknowledged them as divine truth, —— the authority of the evangelists remained the same.   It was even superior ; for a number of *documents*, acknowledged by all parties as the truth of God, would, inevitably, carry more weight with them, than the mere *verbal message* of one individual, even though professedly sent by an apostle.   This latter

---

* 2 Tim. iii. 16, 17, and iv. 1, 2.

might be a forgery, or it might be a mistake, but there could be no forgery, no mistake in the former; for, among the people to whom they originally came from the apostles, usually accompanied by a number of messengers, they always remained the same; and hence the whole of these documents possessed the highest degree of evidence, when formed into a volume. The chief difference, then, between the ancient missionary and the modern, is, the *one* had the *oral* instructions of the apostles, and the *other* has their written testimony. When all these circumstances, then, are considered, we see the amount of the authority of the evangelists in the churches. They could ordain none but those whom the churches elected. They could rebuke by no authority, but the authority of revelation; and their carrying a verbal message from the apostles, amounts, in fact, to less weight, unless proved by their other endowments, than carrying the whole scriptures does now.

Besides, if we examine the matter in point of fact, we shall find, that in some of the churches, the authority of the evangelists, as the messengers of the apostles, and the authority even of the apostles themselves, were, occasionally, at least, very small. This was the case with even the most distinguished of them. How soon did the whole of the churches in the province of Galatia, revolt from under the guidance of the apostle Paul? What address had he to put forth, in the letter he wrote them, in order to bring them to a right state of mind? Look also at Corinth, and the factions into which it was rent? In consequence of these, they only acknowledged him in part; that is, a part of them only acknowledged him, and treated him as they ought to have done. * As the result of all this, mark the way in which he speaks of Timothy, as having gone among them as the bearer of his first epistle. "Now," says he, "if Timotheus come,

---

* 2 Cor. i. 14.

D 3

see that he may be with you *without fear*, for he work-
eth the work of the Lord, even as I also do.   Let no
man, therefore, *despise* him; but *conduct* him forth in
peace, that he may come unto me, for I look for him
with the brethren." *   Now, surely, among a people to
whom such an advice was necessary, Timothy could exert but little authority, even though he might have had
a high portion of it elsewhere.   The apostles, indeed,
had an authority to curb such abuses, namely, the apostolic rod, but this they could not delegate to others.
To this Paul refers, in the same letter, " What will ye ?"
says he, " Shall I come unto you with a rod, or in love,
or in the spirit of meekness ?"   This, however, was the
last resort of an apostle, and hence he never had recourse
to it, till all his influence as a spiritual father, and all his
authority as God's ambassador, had failed.   The evangelists, however, had no such authority ; at least, that
we ever read of.   It seems one of the signs peculiar to
an apostle. †

In speaking of the authority of the evangelists, there
is also another consideration not to be forgotten ; there
were individuals, in all the churches, *equal*, and some
of them *superior*, to themselves.   The pastors and
teachers were their equals, in point of endowment, and
the prophets were their superiors.   It is not likely, then,
that they would come to the churches, with any authority over these, distinct from that which was involved in
a verbal message, delivered by them from the apostles.
What is to be understood, then, by the *authority* that
they are evidently called to exercise ?   It includes, we

---

* 1 Cor. xvi. 10, 11.

† The exercise of the apostolic rod is seen in the case of Ana-
nias and Sapphira, as by it they were struck dead by Peter ; and
also of Elymas the sorcerer, who was struck with blindness by
Paul ; and of Hymeneus and Alexander, who, by Paul, were delivered to Satan, that they might learn not to blaspheme.   See
Acts v. 1-11 ; xiii. 8-11 ; and 1 Tim. i. 20.

apprehend, the following things: first, to co-operate with the prophets, pastors, and teachers, who held the truth, in opposing the errors of false teachers. This Timothy would do, in the case of Hymeneus, Philetus, &c. Secondly, their authority would include their reproving whatever was sinful, in the practice of those who, professedly, held the truth, whether official or non official. This Titus is called to do, with regard to the Cretians. Thirdly, their authority would appear in delivering the apostolic mandates, respecting the formation of new churches, and the setting in order the things that were wanting. All this, however, is only, as we have seen, the authority of revelation, and is an authority which is often *inculcated* on modern ministers, both pastors and missionaries, and also *exercised* by them, without the thought ever entering their minds, that they were called to exercise, or had exercised, either an almost, or a delegated, apostolic authority.

SECTION FIFTH.

The extent of the usefulness of the evangelists:

First, in the world.

Their usefulness, in the first place, had respect to the *world.* Their office, indeed, had especial respect to it, as the office of pastor had respect to the *church.* During the first Century, they were most extensively useful, in almost every part of the Roman Empire. At that time, it is highly probable, there would be no city, and scarcely a town, or even a village, without a Christian church. The spread of Methodism and Dissent, in our own country and America, during the last century, and the success which has attended the foreign missions during the last fifty years, are proofs, to guide us in our conclusions, on this head. The field of success seems, however, to have been, principally, in the more cultivated and thickly inhabited countries, around the great basin of the Mediterranean, from Persia, on the east, to the pillars of Hercules, on the west ; and from Scythia, the Euxine, and Gaul, on the north, to Ethiopia, and the great desert of Africa, on the south. Could we calculate the number of cities and towns, in this part of the Empire, leaving out entirely the pagani, or the villagers, and striking an average of the probable degree of success in each, we should be able, pretty nearly, to ascertain the number of churches, and even Christians, at that time, in the world, — being the first fruits from among the children of men unto God. Paul and Peter died before the year seventy, but John, and Timothy, and Clemens Romanus, supposed to be the Clemens referred to by Paul, in his epistle to the Philippians ; and, perhaps, several others of the apostolic labourers, lived till about the end of the first century. These latter, in beholding the degree of success which had attended their labours, would, when leaving the world, have scarcely a single wish left uncrowned ; and, would, cheerfully, descend into their graves with the words of Simeon on their lips, " now, Lord, lettest thou thy servants depart in peace, for our eyes have seen thy salvation."

Second, in the churches.

The usefulness of these primitive missionaries was equally great in the church, as it was in the world. Its principal feature, however, was, the circumstance of *binding all the different churches together by the holy band of Christian union.* These churches, in themselves, were all *separate* and *independent* bodies. This independency chiefly consisted in the following particulars : the choice of their office bearers, — the admission and expulsion of their members, and the control of their contributions. As to the first of these, it is evident, from what has been already stated, respecting the selection of bishops and deacons. As to the acceptation of members, churches were called upon to receive those only that sustained a certain character, and that character included repentance towards God, and faith towards our Lord Jesus Christ. In this way, Christ receives each, and, in this way, they are commanded to receive one another. "Wherefore," says the apostle, "receive ye one another, as Christ received us, to the glory of God."[*] As to the expulsion of members, the course to be pursued is clear, from the law of discipline laid down by our Lord. The last stage of that discipline, is stated in the following terms : "If he will not hear the church, let him be unto thee as a heathen man and a publican."[+] As to the control of their contributions, the liberty of each church, in this point, is seen, in the manner in which Paul addresses the church at Corinth, on the principle of liberality. In enjoining this on them, he levies no tax, but leaves the performance of the duty, the amount of it, its final destination, and those who are to conduct it to that destination, entirely to themselves. An *object* of bounty might be, indeed, presented, and recommended at that period, by any one, *without* the church. He might also suggest principles, tending to guide the amount of it ; and might also advert to the best time of collecting it, and the method best adapted to carry it to where it was needed ; — but, still, all was left to the church's own generosity and Christian principle. [‡] There was no *control* from *without* ; no interference, on the part of one church with another, in any of the above points. In each, and all of the primitive churches — so far as we have an opportunity of judging from the New Testament,—each church was independent of every other. This is corroborated by the testimony of Mosheim, who says, "The churches, in those times,

---

[*] Rom. xv. 7.　　[+] Matt. viii. 17.　　[‡] 2 Cor. chapters viii. ix.

were entirely independent ; none of them was subject to any foreign jurisdiction, but each was governed by its own rulers." * — Lord King, also, says, " that every particular church had power to exercise discipline on its own members, without the concurrency of other churches." † Gibbon, also, affirms, when speaking of the constitution of the primitive churches, — That " every society formed within itself an independent republic."‡

But while the churches, on these points, acted on the principle of independency, this was a principle on which *alone* they did not act. There was another which also guided them, and that was the principle of union. Each church, indeed, looked upon itself as a separate and independent battalion, but still they regarded themselves as attached to other separate and independent battalions, and each and all of these composing one great army, under the guidance of one skilful and powerful chief. Or to change the metaphor, to one more common in the scriptures, namely, to that of a body and its different members. — Each of the members of a body, we know has its separate and independent functions, but all these functions, of these separate members, contribute by their combination, toward the benefit of the whole frame. So is it with that body, of which Christ is the head. Its separate parts are intended to act in harmony, for the benefit of the whole. Such, indeed, is the natural tendency of genuine Christianity. It leads to love and unity; hence says the apostle to the Thessalonians, " But as touching brotherly love, ye need not that I write unto you, for ye yourselves are taught of God to love one another." ‖ Every real Christian, then, will seek the well-being of the

---

* Ecclesiastical History, Cent. i. chap 2.
† Enquiry into the constitution of the primitive churches, &c. page 136, 138, Edition 1712. ‡ Decline and Fall, Chap. xv. Sec. 5.
‖ 1 Thess. iv. 9.

church with which he is connected; and suppose a church to be composed of such individuals, must it not seek, inevitably, the welfare of all other churches?—For the unity of all his followers, our Lord himself, most fervently prayed, and that in order to the conversion of the world. Every man, then, who has imbibed his spirit, must do the same, for "if we have not the spirit of Christ we are none of his."— Christians, also, are called upon to co-operate with each other, in carrying forward the cause of their Redeemer; hence Paul calls on the Philippians to "strive together for the faith of the gospel." * And the exhortation he gives to one church, he gives, in substance, to a group of churches, to be attended to, not only in their individual capacities, but as churches, one to another. "Bear ye," says Paul to the Galatians, "one another's burdens, and so fulfil the law of Christ." "Let us not be weary in well-doing,"—"as we have therefore opportunity, let us do good unto all men, especially unto them who are of the household of faith." † — Besides, the first churches expressed their love, unity, and co-operation with each other, in various ways. They recognised each other, as churches, by sending their salutations one to another, "The churches of Christ salute you," said Paul to the Romans; and to the Corinthians, he says, "the churches of Asia salute you." ‡ When the members of one church left their brethren on any particular errand, they were recommended to another, as in the case of Phebe, by the church at Cenchrea, to the church at Rome. The more junior churches asked instruction from the more senior, respecting their obedience to God, in certain particulars, as in the case of the church at Antioch, and those of Syria in general, inquiring of the church at Jerusalem, where the apostles then were, respecting the

---

* Phil. i. 27.　　　† Gal. vi. 2, 9, 10.　　　‡ Romans xvi. 16,
and 1 Cor. xvi. 19.

duty of the Gentile churches, in the case of circumcision. * Sometimes, also, they sent spiritual assistance to one another; as the church at Jerusalem to the church at Antioch; and sometimes temporal, as the church of Antioch, in the time of the dearth, to the church at Jerusalem. † —— Other instances might be specified, but these may suffice to shew, that the principle of union was not only possessed, but acted on.

Now the principal instruments of promoting this union were the evangelists; and they did so, in a variety of ways. In the first place, they did so, by adopting every means to keep alive the *spirit* of union among the churches. A number of bodies may be professedly united, but what signifies their apparent union, when the spirit of it is gone? The spirit of patriotism, or loyalty, is an essential engredient, in a conquering army. It was *this*, more than *numbers*, that gained the day at Marathon, at Bannockburn, and Agincourt. It was the spirit of union, also, that rendered the first Christians victorious over their bitterest foes. Hence, of the church at Jerusalem, it is said, "that the multitude of them that believed, were of one heart and one soul, and great grace was upon them all; —— therefore the apostles, with *great power*, gave witness of the resurrection of the Lord Jesus." ‡ —— To preserve this spirit of union, then, in its highest vigour, was one prime object in the ministrations of the evangelists, among the churches; and the method they adopted was, *to preserve them sound in the faith*. They knew well that soundness in the faith lay at the root of every right feeling, and every right action. They knew well, that unless men continue attached to the cross of Christ, they will not continue attached either to his person, or to the furtherance of the interests of his kingdom. To keep them sound in the faith, then, they regarded as

---

* Acts xv. 1-29.   † Acts xi. 22-30.   ‡ Acts iv. 32, 33.

absolutely necessary to their maintaining in vigour the spirit of union among Christians. As the feeling of loyalty in an army, is the grand spring of its union, so is attachment to the work and person of Christ, the great source of all real union among Christians. Without this, all appearance of union would only be a name. To preserve this, then, the first missionaries evinced, *in their own persons, ardent attachment to the Saviour.* "What things were gain to me," says Paul, "those I counted loss for Christ," &c. * And he also calls on Timothy to maintain the unfeigned faith that was in him, by being an example to the believers in faith, as well as in word, conversation, charity, spirit, and purity. † The evangelists endeavoured to preserve the spirit of union, also, *by their own preaching.* Hence Titus is called upon "to be a *pattern* of good works," and "in doctrine, to shew uncorruptness — sound speech, also, that could not be condemned, that he that was of the contrary part might be ashamed." ‡ Hence their opposition, in general, to false teachers. Hence the stern resistance that Paul gave to such persons, in the case of the Galatians. "As we said before, so say I now again, if any man preach any other gospel unto you than that ye have received, let him be accursed." Hence the decided part Paul took in opposition to Peter at Antioch, when he was about to compromise the doctrine of salvation by grace. He knew, that attachment to the cross was the very life's blood of Christianity — that, if it were gone, farewell to all love to Christ — all love to his people, and all hearty co-operation in carrying on his cause. Lastly, the evangelists would endeavour to secure this object, by *the share they held in the appointment of pastors.* They would know that teacher and taught usually resemble each other. As they had a veto, then, upon the appointment of

---

* Phil. iii. 7, 8.   † 1 Tim. iv. 12.   ‡ Titus ii. 7, 8.

E

the office of bishop, they would exercise this, so as to prevent any being ordained, who held erroneous sentiments respecting the gospel. * In these ways, then, would the evangelists exert themselves, to maintain the *spirit* of *unity*, among the early Christians; assured, that unless there were to them "one Lord, one faith, one baptism, one God and Father of all, who is above all, and through all, and in them all," they would not long remain a united people.

But these evangelists were useful in promoting unity among Christians, by their *removals from one place to another, and, consequently, by their frequent visitations to the churches.* — We have seen that they had different districts allotted to them, and that from time to time, they were removed from these. One result of this would be, that one church would hear what was the state of other churches, and thus be led to sympathise with them. Such is the case, with the removals of either home or foreign missionaries, of modern times. Who has not been a thousand-fold more interested, in the spiritual well-being of distant nations and churches, by hearing accounts respecting them, from those that have been, previously, labourers among them? Like circumstances must ever produce corresponding effects. What an interest must have been felt in the church at Philippi, when Timothy related the account of the conversion of the Jailor and his family? This, however, would only be one instance among many.

Epistolary correspondence was another way in which the first missionaries promoted the unity of the churches. The apostles acted thus, and, doubtless, with great effect. They could not always be present with the churches they had planted, but whether present, or absent, they were deeply interested in their spiritual

---

* 1 Tim. v. 22.

well-being; and when they heard that any of them, by the cunning sleight of men, had been moved away from the hope of the gospel, if they could not go to them in person, they wrote letters to them. Such was the case with Paul, in reference to the Galatians; and though we know not precisely the effect produced, there is every reason to believe that the letters written to them, would not be sent in vain. We have certain evidence that this was the case with the Corinthians. In his first letter to them, Paul reproved them sharply, for their conduct, in the case of the incestuous person, and it had the desired effect upon the minds of the church, and also on the party alluded to. It wrought in both, "godly sorrow," which led to "repentance which needed not to be repented of." From this, is it not reasonable to conclude, that his second letter would lead to the most happy results, in producing among them the spirit of liberality? In the letters thus sent, there were also, usually contained, a number of salutations from the church, or churches, in the neighbourhood where the writer was then labouring; and also from particular individuals, in these churches. Now all this was well adapted to produce the most pleasing effect, on the minds of the parties to whom these greetings were sent. The expression of affection usually enkindles the same feeling, in the minds of those to whom it is manifested. Now such being the conduct of the master, is it not likely that in this he would be imitated by his pupils? If Paul wrote thus to the churches, to cherish the spirit of unity, and actually to maintain it in the churches, it is but reasonable to suppose that Timothy and others would do the same. We have, indeed, no remains of such letters; but the letters of Ignatius and Polycarp, render it extremely probable, that the primitive evangelists did the same. The circumstance, also, of Clemens Romanus writing his epistle, in the name of the church at Rome to the church at Corinth, makes it a likely matter that this was not uncommon with others of the apostolic labourers, as well as with him. If so, this would most materially tend to unite the two societies — the society writing, and the society written to.

The begetting a spirit of sympathy, in the different churches, towards each other, was also another way in which these good men promoted their unity. Paul and Barnabas did this, in the case of the churches of Phenice and Samaria, when they declared to them the conversion of the Gentiles. It is said, the circumstance gave "great joy to all the brethren." * At another time, Paul used all his influence, in the Gentile churches, to induce them to send relief to the poor saints at Jerusalem. His object appears to have been, not merely to give relief to these sufferers, but to promote the most kindly feeling between the Jewish and Gentile Christians. He wished to bind them to each other, by begetting the feeling of gratitude in both, towards each other. He wished to promote it in the breasts of the Gentiles to the Jews, on account of their ministering to them, in spiritual things ; and in the breasts of the Jews, to the Gentiles, because of their ministering to them in carnal things. † In this, the apostle succeeded ; at least, so far as the Gentiles were concerned. All the churches in Galatia and Phrygia, and, in all likelihood, the whole of the other churches in Asia Minor, together with the churches in Macedonia and Achaia, were imbued, by him and his fellow labourers, with the spirit of liberality ; and some of them, from their love to the Saviour, and his people, in the depth of their poverty, contributed most abundantly toward the object intended. ‡

There was also another way, in which the missionary brethren of that day, became the instruments of promoting intercourse between the churches. This was by

---

* Acts xv. 3.   † Rom. xv. 25-27   ‡ 2 Cor. viii. 1-4, &c.

becoming their messengers, on special occasions. Such
was the case with Peter and John, when deputed by
the church at Jerusalem, to go and assist at the religious awakening produced at Samaria, through the
means of Philip; * and such was the case also with
Barnabas, when on a like occasion, he was sent, by
the same church, to Antioch. The one people could
not but see the deep interest taken in their spiritual
welfare, on these occasions, by the other; and this
must have produced the most happy and uniting effect
upon their minds. When the relief already referred
to, was sent from the Gentile churches, to the poor
saints at Jerusalem, a number of these same men were
sent, by the churches, with their bounty. Paul was,
doubtless, placed at the head of this deputation, and
Luke, and Timothy, and others, were appointed to go
with him. There is one circumstance mentioned respecting one of the messengers, supposed to be Luke,
which is well worthy of especial notice, as indicating
the intercourse which sometimes occured between the
churches. It is said, 2 Cor. viii. 19, that he " *was* CHOSEN
OF THE CHURCHES, *to travel with their bounty* to
Jerusalem, along with Paul. Here, then, was an *act*
not of *one* church *only*, but of *several in concert*. Now
the question is, how was this act performed? When
churches were widely separated, as was the case with
these, though in the same province, namely, Macedonia,
it was not an easy thing to consult *unitedly*, about any
particular matter. They are, however, represented as
doing so here. How, then, was it done? Is it un-
reasonable to suppose that they did so by delegation?
Is it unlikely that they sent this delegation to some
central part of the country, where one of the churches
was, and there deliberated together as to who were
to be their messengers to Jerusalem; and having so

* Acts viii. 14, and xi. 22.

F 3

deliberated, that they fixed on Paul and Luke, and, it may be, others with them? The matter is far from being improbable; and not only so, but it seems equally probable, from other circumstances about to be mentioned, that such meetings might not be unfrequent. If so, then from the churches employing these evangelists as messengers, on special occasions, together with the apostles, they became the means of promoting unity and intercourse.

The last thing we shall now mention as contributing to this intercourse, on the part of the evangelists, was, *their own support*. With regard to this support, they enjoyed it, in the first place, in the way of hospitality. Hence the twelve, and the seventy, when sent out by our Lord, were called upon to enquire, wherever they went, for one that was worthy, or a son of peace,—— that is, either a lover of the gospel of peace, or else one well disposed to it; —— and when they had found one such, they were to enter into his house; and there abide, enjoying, with him, all the rights of hospitality. * Our Lord himself was often entertained in the same way, and so were his disciples after his ascension. Peter, we find, the guest of one Simon a Tanner, and Paul was the guest of Lydia, Gaius, and others. Gaius is also said, to have testified his " love to the truth," by " helping " the missionary brethren that came to his neighbourhood, " on their journey, after a godly sort; " and thus he showed himself to be a " fellow helper of the truth." The brethren themselves took nothing from the Gentiles, and provided they were penniless themselves, their only resource then was, the house of a son of peace,—— or professor of the gospel. † But it was not merely by hospitality that the first missionaries were supported; they were so, likewise, by contribu-

---

* Mat. x. 11-14, and Luke x.5-7   † John iii. 5 8.

tion. It is true, the seventy, as well as the twelve, were to take out with them neither purse nor *scrip*; but our Lord himself, and his disciples, were in the habit, generally, of using both. Hence it is said he had a *bag*, that is a *purse*, for there was money in it. This is evident, from what is said respecting it. Our Lord is represented as saying to the traitor, "that thou doest do quickly." It is added, "Now no man at the table knew for what intent he spake this unto him, for some of them thought, because Judas had the bag, that Jesus had said unto him, Buy those things that we have need of against the feast, or that he should give something to the poor." * At another time, we are told, "the disciples were gone to the city to buy meat." † —Here both purse and scrip were required, The purse to buy the meat, and the scrip to hold it. Whence our Lord obtained this supply for his purse, we are not told. The more wealthy of his disciples would, doubtless, contribute to support it; and, perhaps, his disciples sold their all, when they took up their cross, and followed him. Be this as it may, they had a common fund, and this is the first missionary fund we are acquainted with. The common fund of the church at Jerusalem, was, perhaps, only a prolongation of it. The command of our Lord to the seventy, must have had something *special* about it, or else, if attended to in *one* thing, it must be attended to in *all.* A missionary, then, whatever might be his exigences, could not have two coats, &c. Perhaps the reason of the injunction was, not only to teach the twelve, and the seventy, the *unmitigable urgency* attendant on their engagements, but that in the *barest possible condition*, their *real wants* would be still supplied. Their future prospects, doubtless, required such training. The apostles, and other primitive missionaries, however, did not confine

---

* John xiii. 27-29　　† John iv. 8.

themselves to mere hospitality; they also accepted of the contributions of believers, whether in money or in goods. This would depend on the habits of the people among whom they lived. Paul, for example, accepted of the hospitality of Publius at Melita, who, it is said, received them and lodged them courteously three days." The people of the island, also, who had been healed by Paul, as was also the father of Publius, along with him, honoured them with many honours: perhaps the meaning is, as in other places, bestowed upon them many gifts; * and when the apostle and his company departed, the same parties " loaded them with such things as were necessary."

Here, then, were the two ways in which the first missionaries were supported; and this support was commanded by divine authority. Hence our Lord said, when he sent out the seventy, " *The labourer is worthy of his meat, and his hire.*" † This command, in all likelihood, Paul refers to when he says, " *Even so, hath the Lord ordained, that they who preach the gospel shall live of the gospel.*" ‡ Here, then, is the *law* of the case; and no law can possibly be more unequivocally stated. As to those on whom it is obligatory, — these, in the nature of things, can only be expected to be those who feel its force, and acknowledge the authority of the lawgiver; hence, though the missionaries went forth, taking nothing of the Gentiles, they were helped on their way, by Christians, the sons of peace, after a godly sort. It is true, these missionaries did not always take the maintenance from Christians, that their master allowed them to claim. Paul tells the Corinthians, that he had not done so, and would not do so in their case; and he states the reason, namely, " *that he might not hinder the gospel.*" ‖ On the same principle he con-

---

* Acts xxviii. 10, compared with 1 Tim. v. 34, & xvii. 18.
† Matt. x. 10, and Luke x. 7.   ‡ I Cor. ix. 4-14.   ‖ I Cor. ix. 15.

ducted himself, at Ephesus and Thessalonica. * This, however, ought to be regarded as only the *expediency* of the case. There were many things lawful to the a-postle, as he tells us, but these *lawful* things were not always *expedient*. This was the case with him, in re-gard both to eating meat, and to marriage. It was law-ful for him both to eat meat and to marry ; but, for the sake of his ' *weak brethren*,' he would not do the one, and on account of the ' *present distress*,' he abstained from the other. † So with regard to his being main-tained by the gospel, he, on occasions, would not accept of maintenance ; not that it was unlawful, but, in these cases, inexpedient, lest he should hinder the progress of the gospel. The law of the case, then, and its expe-diency, ought ever, in reasoning on this subject, to be carefully discriminated.

From these statements, then, it plainly appears to have been the duty of all the churches of the saints, to sup-port the missionaries, in their arduous labours of itine-rating with the gospel. All the churches, however, did not do so. This was the case at least at Corinth ; and Paul, in writing to the Philippians, says, "now ye Philippians know also, that in the beginning of the gos-pel. no church communicated with me, as concerning giving and receiving, but ye only." Here, then, evi-dently, is a reflection on the churches referred to. It was as much their duty to communicate with the apos-tles, as the Philippians ; but they did not do so. The Philippians, however, did their duty ; and it was " an odour of a sweet smell, a sacrifice well pleasing unto God." ‡ It was so, because they did what God had com-manded, or ordained, in the churches, respecting the maintenance of his ministers. The Lord will honour them that honour him ; and they who despise him shall be

---

* Acts xx. 34, and 1 Thess. ii. 5-10
† 1 Cor. vii. 26, and x. 23.   ‡ Phil. iv. 15-19.

lightly esteemed. Where the churches did not support these labourers, one evil would accrue, namely, the lack of *one band* to unite them. The Macedonians, however, who were linked together by other bands, were linked together by this also. Hence, we are told, that when Paul was at Corinth, and " wanted "——the brethren from Macedonia came and supplied him. * We have seen that these churches, in the case of sending a messenger to Jerusalem, with their bounty, were drawn to a united act in this selection. It would be the same, doubtless, on *this occasion;* and not only so, but, as the support of the missionaries was a constant matter, so their meeting by delegation, to send messengers to supply their wants, would, in all likelihood, render such meetings periodical, and not occasional, as was the case with regard to the poor saints at Jerusalem. Each church would be a missionary society, and all these churches — Philippi, Thessalonica, and Berea — at least, would combine, and meet — thus increasing their union — to choose and send messengers to the missionaries, with the supplies they raised.

Thus, in all these different ways, were the apostles and their assistants, the evangelists, the means of cementing and maintaining union among the churches; and this union they would maintain, not only in the body aggregate, but in its individual parts. If we glance at the epistles to Timothy and Titus, we shall find they would have many opportunities of healing breaches in particular churches. It is hinted that collisions might take place, at times, between the elders and the members of the churches. These latter might, at times, have "itching ears," and so " heap up to themselves, teachers." They might, also, not like certain doctrines, but be turned to fables. In such cases, the missionary could advert to circumstances,

---

* 2 Cor xi. 7-10.

which the elders might feel a delicacy in mentioning. So with regard to the maintenance of any of these elders, that required it. The evangelist could touch on this matter, if the church was defective in their duty, better than the elders themselves, and remind them, that they "who rule well are worthy of double *honour* — even as the scripture saith — "thou shalt not muzzle the ox that treadeth the corn," and "the labourer is worthy of his *reward*." Reward, and honour, then, are here the same. On the other hand, if any of the elders had done what was wrong, the missionaries could assist the church in investigating the matter. Here, however, they were required to act with the greatest caution. Against an elder, they were not to receive an accusation, but before two or three witnesses. When the evidence was, however, substantiated, they were to act with impartiality and decision. "Them that sin, rebuke before all, that others also may fear."— In various other ways, were the missionaries useful in the churches, but these, as a sample, may suffice. They would, doubtless, occasionally meet resistance. The pastors, at times, might not relish their visits, and some Diotrephes might not choose to receive them, jealous of the diminution of his own authority, and might cast out those members that would. But these might be rare instances; and wherever the true spirit of Christianity prevailed in the churches, the presence of the evangelists would be hailed with delight.

Thus, have we considered the *nature* of the office of an evangelist, including a view of the character of his work — the nature of his qualifications — his call and designation,— his authority in the churches,— and his usefulness both in the church and in the world. In doing this, we have classed such persons, as missionaries, along with the apostles. They had not, indeed, the same gift — the word of wisdom, or revelation;— they could not wield the apostolic rod; and, perhaps, they never conferred on any the spiritual *gifts*; all these were, what are termed, the *signs* of an apostle;—but, as far as missionary work, properly so called, was concerned, they stood on the same footing. In *this work*, they were their assistants, while living, and their successors when dead. Like them, *as itinerants*, *they preached the gospel.* Like them, they planted and watered churches; by these churches, like them, they were supported; and like them, they were under the Redeemer, the great links of the chain that bound these churches together.—— Their work was great, arduous, glorious; and they nobly achieved it. Such men the world — the church — never beheld.—— The world despised them, and the church did not always treat them as she should have done; but their unaffected yet ardent piety—their unwearied labours—their prudent zeal —and their heroic bravery and contempt of dangers, and privations, and death, have made their names imperishable. The time will come when the name of the conqueror, who waded to a throne through seas of blood, will rot; but the fragrant memories of the messengers of the prince of peace shall be blessed, and their name held in everlasting remembrance. It will be our object, in the following pages, to ascertain whether or not their office, in the church, was intended to be as enduring as their renown.

PART SECOND.

THE ENQUIRY, WHETHER THE OFFICE OF EVANGE-
LIST WAS INTENDED TO BE A PERMANENT ONE.

SECTION FIRST.

The principle of ascertaining the perpetuity of any office under the Christian dispensation.

The close analogy subsisting between Christianity and Judaism, must be a matter very obvious to even a very cursory observer. The priests, the sacrifices, the ablutions of the one, are so many pictorial representations of the great facts and doctrines of the other. Christianity has its priest, its sacrifice, its means of purification. Its author is both its priest, and its sacrifice ; and his gracious spirit of promise is the grand agent in the purification of the hearts of men. These were "the good things to come." The mosaic priests, and sacrifices, and ablutions, were only their "shadows." A shadow, however, is a likeness : there was a close analogy between them.

But while such is the case, in general, between the two dispensations, there is one point in which there is scarcely any resemblance whatever. That point is, *minute directions regarding particular matters*. Almost every office and institution, under the mosaic economy, had directions given respecting it ; which forcibly re-

F

mind us of the highly appropriate characteristic of the church, in that age, given by the apostle, namely, that of a state of pupilage.* The church then, was, as it were, in a state of childhood ; and, in consequence, directions of the most minute description were given it, to show it the way in which it ought to go. On the contrary, under the Christian dispensation, for the most part, the mere outline respecting institutions and offices is given, with general principles to guide us, in the filling of it up. An instance or two may be referred to, in respect to both dispensations, by way of illustration. In the case of the high priest, under the Jewish economy, how minute are the directions given respecting him and his office ! He must be free from bodily defect ; he must not marry a widow ; he must not be defiled for the dead ; nor mourn, except for the nearest relations ; he must be arrayed in splendid vestments ; and present certain sacrifices, in a particular way, at certain given periods. † These circumstances may serve as a specimen, but they are only a specimen, of the minutiæ, connected with his office. Now, contrast all this with what is said of the office of bishop, in the New Testament. A few verses contain all that is specified, respecting what he ought to be, in order to his being selected to hold the office ; ‡ and his particular duties are to be learned, from the title given him, and the incidental directions, of a general description, strewed here and there, in the acts of the apostles, and the different epistles. The *perpetuity* of the office of the priest, is stated distinctly ; ‖ but nothing is said of the *permanence* of the office of a bishop. The permanence of the office is, however, inferred, and we think justly, from the following obvious considerations, namely, that it is an office *needed* in all times ; and that the natural and moral qualifications specified, in order to

---

* Gal. iv. 1-3　† Levit. Chapters 21 and 22.　‡ 1 Tim. iii. 1-7.
‖ Exod. xxix. 9.

the performance of its duties, are qualifications, that may be possessed at any period. The circumstance, also, of the churches, in different places, being under the superintendance of such a class of officers, shews that it is the intention of the great Christian legislator, that such should be the case with all collections of Christians, in every place, and in every future age of the world.

In all these circumstances, then, if we have not a direct command, we have fair legitimate inferences, respecting the permanence of the office of pastor, elder, or bishop, in a Christian church; and not only so, but we have presented to us the PRINCIPLE, which leads to the ascertainment of the permanence, or non-permanence, of any other office. If, then, there are circumstances, equally clear, and equally numerous, connected with the office of evangelist, to establish its perpetuity; it seems but fair, that the one officer should be regarded equally as permanent, in the church, as tho other. This, we apprehend, can be viewed as only a candid conclusion, if the following considerations can be established, as *facts*, respecting the office in question. If tho *work* of the evangelist is equally as needful, and as much commanded, in all times, as that of a pastor; if the same objections against the continuance of the evangelist's office, are equally valid against the continuance of the pastoral office; if the same qualifications, natural and moral, are called for, in the case of the evangelists, as in the case of bishops; together with a variety of other circumstances, intimating that it is the intention of the head of the church, to continue the one office as well as the other;—then, from these scriptural premises, we may safely conclude, that we are right, in assigning permanence, equally, to both institutions. But if, in addition to all this, we find the office of evangelist actually continued in the best period of the church, after the apostolic age, namely, the second and third centuries; if we find its improper use, or its absolute abeyance, in the following centuries, till after the reformation, arose more from moral causes, in the professors of religion, than from any proof that its exercise was unlawful ; if we find ourselves obliged to regard the office of the modern missionary, in consequence of having no scriptural prototype, rather a human device, than a divine institute ; and, finally, if we find it necessary, in order to the fulfilment of the divine promises, that a class of divinely instituted officers should be appointed, to carry them into effect ; then we shall see increased reason to recognise the permanent institution of the evangelists' office, as well as the pastoral. We shall endeavour, in the following sections, to make the truth of all these various points apparent.

SECTION SECOND.

The genius of Christianity ; the commission of Christ ; the wisdom of God ; and the character of the work and situation of the Christian pastor, as well as the other primitive labourers ; shew the necessity of a continued class of missionary labourers, in all succeeding ages.

The genius, or leading characteristic of Christianity is, the exhibition of a remedy, for the salvation of a lost world. "God so loved the world, that He gave his only begotten Son, that whosoever believeth in him should not perish, but have everlasting life." The heart and soul of love and mercy, are embraced in these expressions. The being who uttered them, felt these in all their fervour. Yearning over the salvation of the immortal spirit of the ruler of the Jews, whom he was then addressing, all that is charming, — all that is lovely,— all that is truly characteristic of Christianity, would, in his sacred countenance, at that time, be depicted. The same feeling, in kind, though immeasurably less, in degree, is experienced, by all those, who have any personal acquaintance with his "saving health." No evidence can be more sure, of any one having found salvation to his own soul, than the circumstance of hi seeking, with assiduity, after the salvation of the souls of others. This may, assuredly, be set down, as the inevitable characteristic of a truly healthy state of the soul of man. Whoever does not feel thus, and does not act under the influence of such feeling, is in possession of sufficient evidence, that his heart is not right with God. If he can allow day after day to pass, and give no annoyance to those around him, that are sleeping secure in their sins ; if there is nothing of the feeling of a missionary within him, or the doings of a missionary manifested by him ; if there is nothing in him akin to the spirit of the great missionary, who came all the way from heaven to earth, to seek and to save the lost ; then, there is reason, deep reason, to suspect, either that he has never known the truth, or, if he has so, that his heart has grievously backslidden from God.

When we look to the experience of the truly pious, presented to us in the sacred volume, we find that the state of their hearts was truly missionary. The book of Psalms, is replete with expressions to this effect. " Rivers of waters run down mine eyes because they keep not thy law." " God be merciful to us, and bless us, and cause thy face to shine upon us, that thy way may be known upon earth, thy saving health among all nations." " His name shall endure for ever; his name shall be continued as long as the sun ; men shall be blessed in him; and all nations shall call him blessed.— And blessed be his glorious name for ever; and let the whole earth be filled with his glory;" Amen, and Amen. In the New Testament, the same exquisite tone of missionary feeling prevails. How strikingly does this appear, in the first disciples of our Lord ! How beautifully simple is the story respecting Andrew the brother of Peter, originally a disciple of the Baptist ! How characteristic of genuine Christian and missionary feeling! John stood with two of his disciples, we are told, and looking upon Jesus as he walked, said, " behold the Lamb of God." " And the disciples heard him speak, and they followed Jesus. Then Jesus turned and saw them following, and saith to them, what seek ye? They said Rabbi — where dwellest thou? He saith unto them, come and see. They came and saw, and abode with him that day :"— and, O, what a day must it have been to them! It is added, " one of the two was Andrew." He first findeth his brother Simon, and saith unto him, " We have found the Messias, which is, being interpreted, the Christ." * In this beautifully simple story, we have the genuine operations of a truly converted mind. That mind itself, in the first instance, meets with the Saviour, and then longs to draw all others to him. So with Philip — " He findeth," it is said, " Nathanael and saith unto him, We have found him of whom Moses, in the law and the prophets did write, Jesus of Nazareth, the son of Joseph." † So the woman of Samaria, " Come," said she to her town's-people — " Come, see a man which told me all things that ever I did : is not this the Christ?" ‡ In all this, we perceive the native tendency of Christianity :— and such being its tendency, as thousands of instances, in addition to the above, attest, in every age, we also perceive that the missionary spirit, in the Christian church, so long as true piety exists, can never be extinguished ; and that, consequently, some individuals will ever be found, in every age, disposed, even without directions, to burst every fetter that might be laid upon them, in the way of restraint, and to perform, with zeal, the work of evangelists. Missionary labour, then, we see, springs from the very genius of Christianity.

But, if such is the native tendency of Christianity,

---

* John i. 35-42.   † John i. 43-45.   ‡ John iv. 29.

even independent of any special command on the subject ; — for many act thus, who never think of any
particular scriptural commission to do so, but purely
from the compassionate, generous, and expansive feeling
of Christian benevolence working in the soul ; — how
much more is the proof for the continuance of mission-
ry labour, in the world, increased, when we reflect *on
our Lord's commission?* * That commission involved
the following particulars — namely, first, the proclamation of the gospel ; — " preach," says the Saviour, " the
gospel." The gospel, is the good news of God's mercy to
sinful men, founded on the incarnation, and substitution,
of Jesus Christ. The good news, then, of mercy, *thus
based*, were to be *proclaimed* publicly, and *taught* privately. Secondly, this preaching was to begin at a
particular centre, and that centre was Jerusalem. The
first offer of God's mercy, was to be presented to his
greatest enemies, — to the most hardened — the chief
of sinners — the murderers of Messiah. This, truly,
if any thing can, evinces the genius of Christianity.
Thirdly, it was to spread from Jerusalem, as from a centre, to the wide circumference of the globe. " Go,"
says the Saviour, " into all the world, and preach the
gospel to every creature." Every nation was to be
visited, and every individual taught the way to heaven ;
and to be entreated, in Christ's stead, to walk in that
way. All who obeyed, were to be led into all the
truth as it is in Jesus, and to attend to " all things " he
had commanded ; they who did so, would find their
happiness, both in this world, and in that which is to
come. Fourthly, this commission was given to the
apostles. It was so, because they were peculiarly fitted for the work. They were the witnesses of all the
facts upon which the gospel they were to proclaim, was

---

* Matt. xxviii. 19-20 ;   Mark xvi. 15-16 ;   Luke xxiv. 47-48 ;
and Acts i. 8.

founded.   They had seen Jesus, and been intimately
acquainted with him, before his death; and were all
the chosen witnesses of his resurrection — the grand
fact, which put the crown of truth on all the rest.   In
addition, they were soon to be endowed with extraordinary power, from on high, to qualify them to speak
the different languages of the earth, and to attest, by
astonishing miracles, that all they affirmed was true.
Fifthly, this commission was given, in perpetuity, to the
apostles, as the representatives of the future church of
God, and of the men, whom God, in future, would qualify,
to carry on the same work in the world.   This is evident, from the promise appended to the commission.
" Lo, I am with you alway, even to the end of the
world."   The end of the world, must here mean, the
end of time, the period alluded to by the apostle,
when he says, " Then cometh the end, when he (Christ)
shall have delivered up the Kingdom to God, even the
Father."*   The Kingdom, here referred to, is, doubtless,
the power and dignity with which our Lord was invested, after his resurrection; and to which he alludes,
when he says, "All power is given to me, in heaven,
and in earth; go, therefore, disciple all nations; and lo,
I am with you, and with those who shall succeed you,
till I resign the power, with which I am now invested,
at the end of time."   Such, evidently, appears the
meaning of this promise; and if so, then, it necessa-
rily follows, that the apostles were missionaries; that
their missionary work was not to die with them; but
that when they passed off the stage, other missionaries
would succeed them; and that such should be the case,
in all succeeding ages, till time itself should terminate.
Here, then, is clear proof of the *intention* of Christ,
that MISSIONARY WORK, should be permanent in the
church of God, in all succeeding ages.

---

* 1 Cor. xv. 24.

Now, if missionary *work* was thus to be extended to the end of time, is it not natural to suppose, that *a class of labourers*, adapted to the purpose, would be provided, by the great head of the church? To suppose otherwise, would, inevitably, impugn the only wise God as one who lacked wisdom. Yet such appears to be the case, when we hold the perpetuity of the commission, and deny the perpetuity of the office of evangelist. We have the anomalous circumstance, presented to us for our wonderment, of God prescribing work, and yet allotting no one to perform it! What is this but something like beginning to build, and not being able to finish? — A line of conduct severely reprobated by our Lord himself. Strange, indeed, that he himself should have fallen into it! It may, however, be said, that God has left this work to his especial providence. In reply, it may be mentioned, that this is not the usual mode of the divine procedure: it is true, indeed, that all He appoints to be done, He especially superintends, by his providence; hence, this may be as much affirmed of one divine institution, as of another — of the pastor's office, as well as of the missionary's. It is his providence that furnishes all the churches with pastors. God raises all of them up, and qualifies them, and no church has a right to elect any to be pastors, but those whom God has, previously, elected, by the talents and grace with which he has furnished them. His providence, however, does not supersede the choice of the people; it only goes before it. Neither does the appointment of the office, supersede the operations of divine providence, any more than the operations of divine providence supersede it. God's institutions, and God's providence, are ever found acting in harmony, and are never opposed, the one to the other. The idea, then, of leaving a work to providence alone, that the Lord of providence especially appointed and devolved upon his people, in all succeeding ages, seems to be a mistaken one; and one neither supported by the deductions of reason, nor the statements of the word of God. Nothing, indeed, can be more unlike God, than to appoint work to be done, and make no provision in his word, for its performance. To say the least of it, this is not the usual mode of the divine procedure. In every age, when He had an object in view, He always adopted means, to gain the end. When the object was a transient one, individuals, adapted to the end, were raised up, for the time being. Such were Moses, and Joshua, and Elijah, and others, of a similar description : and when the object was a continuous one, one that was to pass through successive generations — then, corresponding means were employed. God, for instance, determined that, during a lengthened period, his truth should be deposited with a certain people ; and that from that people the Messiah should eventually come ; and the *children* of *Israel* were selected for this purpose. Hence, also, the priesthood, that ran through the long line of Aaron ; and the monarchy, that descended through the family of David. The sceptre was not to depart from Judah, nor a law-giver from between his feet, till Shiloh — the prince of peace — should come.

In all these instances, then, we find the wisdom of God operating, as we might have expected ; appointing ends, and fixing, at the same time, on suitable means to gain them. No idea, then, can be more preposterous, more blasphemous, or, as Mr. Ward expresses it, more profane, than to affirm, that, the great head of the church, should design a work for the salvation of the world, and command that the knowledge of that work should be communicated to all the inhabitants of the world, in every successive generation ; and yet appoint no standing officers, in his church, in order to its accomplishment. No possible libel could be greater upon the wisdom of God, than this. The genius of Christianity, then, the commission of Christ, and the perfection of wisdom in the Deity, all loudly demand, in each successive age of the world, such an office as that of missionary.   But upon which of all the classes of officers, appointed and endowed by our great Redeemer, in the first age of Christianity, did this work devolve?   For the present, this question shall only be answered negatively.   It did not devolve on the *bishops*, or *pastors* of churches.   There are two circumstances connected with the office of a bishop, which may serve to shew, that *he* is not the *officer*, appointed to carry the gospel to every creature.   These are, the *nature of his duties, and the locality of his labour*.   With regard to the first of these — the nature of his duties, — it is obvious, that in all that is said, about the pastoral office, and all that is directed to those who held it, that it was, chiefly, confined to the converted.   Hence, says Paul, to the elders of Ephesus, "Take heed to yourselves, and to all the flock, over which the Holy Ghost hath made you overseers, to feed the church of God, which he hath purchased with his own blood." *   In terms somewhat similar, Peter addresses elders — "The elders which are among you I exhort — Feed the flock of God, which is among you, taking the oversight thereof, not by constraint, but willingly, not for filthy lucre, but of a ready mind.   Neither as being lords over God's heritage, but being ensamples to the flock." †   These exhortations, then, plainly show, that as elders, bishops, or pastors, their work was confined to the church. This appears, also, in the addresses to the churches, with relation to their pastors. "Remember them," says the writer to the Hebrews, "who have the rule over you, who have spoken unto you the word of God; whose faith follow, considering the end of their conversation, &c.   And again, "Obey them that have the rule over you, and submit yourselves: for they watch for your souls, as they that must give an account; that they may do it with joy, and not with grief," &c. ‡

---

* Acts xx. 28.   † 1 Peter v. 1, 2, 3.   ‡ Heb. xiii. 7-17.

When Timothy is called upon to point out the qualifications of a bishop, among other things he is called to state, one is, — "he must be able to govern his own house well; for, unless he did so, how could he take care of the *church of God?*" * The church of God, then, is the peculiar province of the bishop; any bishop, that wishes properly to discharge the duties of his office, as they should be, by instructing, publicly, a church of only moderate dimensions, and catechising them, and visiting them, privately, and attending on the sick, and the aged; will find his time amply employed. In consequence of this, he cannot be intended, by infinite wisdom, to discharge the duty, involved in our Lord's commission, of preaching the gospel to every creature.

But the same may be affirmed, arising from the other consideration, namely, the locality of pastoral labour. A pastor's duties must, inevitably, be confined within a very narrow circumference. Within the range of that circumference, the whole, or, at least the greater number of his flock, reside. To their wants, then, he is chiefly called to attend. And, even supposing, that he sustained in his own person, the double character of pastor and local preacher, still his range of operation must be very limited. If he preached to the ungodly, within the circumference of the locality of his flock, that would be about as large a part of the world, as he could be expected to do justice to, in his present circumstances. Such being the case, then, it must follow, that, if the commission of our Lord is to be fulfiled, it must be by a class of spiritual instructors, distinct from those, who are supposed to be, the only permanent spiritual officers, left to the church.

Who, then, it may still be asked, are these officers? If not among the bishops, where, among all the other

---

* 1 Tim. iii. 5.

original labourers, shall we find them? Shall we find
them among the prophets? We again answer no; and
that for two reasons: first, the nature of their gift,
which involved immediate communication from God,
as in sitting in the church, it is said, they had something *revealed* to them. Unless, then, we had persons
possessing such a gift — the office to which it belonged,
cannot be continued. Again: the nature of the work of
the prophets was not missionary. It related to the
exhortation, edification, or comfort, of the church; and,
therefore, cannot be the work in question. If the work
of the prophet, then, is continued, it is now merged in
the office of pastor. The same also, perhaps, may be
affirmed of another class, who had an extraordinary gift,
at this period. These were they who are termed,
" governments." It has been mentioned, when speaking of the primitive gifts, that these, by some, are supposed to have been those, who had the discernment of
spirits; namely, those who sat and judged — whether
the revelations of the prophets were real, or otherwise.
If such, then, was their office, their work, also, was
stationary, not ambulatory; and peculiar, likewise, to
the age in which they lived. If these were, however,
what some others, from their title, have supposed them
to be, namely, the presidents, or rulers, or pastors, of the
churches, the same thing may still be affirmed. As it
regards those called " helps ;" some have supposed them
to be the evangelists, as they assisted the apostles; others
have supposed them to be the deacons of the churches; who, in various ways, helped the pastors; and
others have supposed them, as already intimated, to be
those who are called "interpreters of tongues." In the
two latter cases, their work is also confined to the
church; and in the former, they are the class whose
pretensions are hereafter to be considered. We may
only mention, in passing, that, regarding these as interpreters of divine revelation from one language into
another, the translators of scriptures among the mis-

G

sionaries, come nearest to these of any others, in modern times.

But was the apostolic office to be continued, and is this not to be regarded as the office especially in question?   To this it may be replied, the apostles were, indeed, ambulatory labourers; and the commission of Christ was, originally, given to them; and as that work was undying, even though they themselves passed off the stage, so it behoved some to take it up, when they were gone.   This part of their work, then, being continuous, they must, in *it*, have successors; but as another part of their work was altogether extraordinary, namely, the revelations which they gave of the divine will, in this part of it they can have no successors. On this account, then, as well as on account of other circumstances, connected with the apostolic office, namely, the signs peculiar to them, elsewhere referred to, it cannot be said, with propriety, that this was the class of officers, who were intended to be employed, by God, in his church, to the end of time.   There is, then, only one other class remaining — the evangelists; and, as they were the assistants of the apostles, in their missionary labours, it remains to be ascertained, whether there was any thing connected with their office, to prevent them from being regarded, in common, with the pastors of Christian churches, as permanent officers, attached to the cause of God, in all succeeding ages. The solution to this enquiry we shall endeavour to give, in the following section.

SECTION THIRD.

There was nothing in the work, qualifications, call, or authority, of the evangelists, as it regards an extraordinary character, inimical to the perpetuity of their office ; any more than to that of the Christian pastor.

It has been frequently affirmed — and this is the idea we are now attempting to combat — that the office of evangelist, was an *extraordinary* one. It may be necessary to make a few preliminary remarks, before directly meeting this assertion. It is necessary, before subscribing to the above statement, to enquire, what an extraordinary office means ? Perhaps, the most comprehensive reply to this question is, — that it is one the work of which is both *peculiar*, and *temporary*. As to its peculiarity, it s so, with regard to its *kind*. This is the case, with respect to the receiving and communicating divine revelation. This was, indeed, a work altogether peculiar, and restricted to the individuals who were called to engage in it. The modes of communicating revelation to these individuals, might vary, but still, their work, in conveying it to men, was one and the same. Such was the case with Moses, in revealing the law. So was it with the prophets, in foretelling future events, with regard either to the rise, or fall of empires, the sufferings of Christ, or the glory that should follow. Such was the case, also, with the apostles, when, under the guidance of the word of wisdom, the extraordinary gift with which they were endowed, they unfolded the glorious mysteries of redemption — the doctrines founded on those facts which they had both seen and heard. And such was the case with the prophets of the Christian church ; the gift of prophecy, raised them far above their brethren, and enabled them, not only to foretell future events, but also to speak in the church, "to edification, exhortation, and comfort." Such, then, was the peculiar character of the work, connected with an extraordinary office. Combined with this, however, there was its temporary character. It was exercised, for a season only, and only appeared at distant intervals; sometimes more; sometimes less. God, at *sundry times*, and in divers manners, spake in times past to the fathers, &c. * From the giving of the law, by Moses, to the completion of the New Testament canon, by the apostle John, a period of nearly two thousand years had passed over the world, during which time, a number of individuals had appeared, at different intervals, all exercising in greater or lesser degree, and in a temporary way, the extraordinary work of communicating the will of God to man.

If such, then, are the features of an extraordinary office, the opposite must be the features of an ordinary one. If the one is peculiar, the other is more common; and, if the one is temporary, the other is permanent. Such was the case with the priests and levites under the law; their office was a permanent one, held in common with many others, belonging to the same tribe, in all succeeding generations, till the end of the Jewish polity. Their work was, indeed, appointed by God, as well as the work of the prophets; but with this difference — what was the work of one priest, was the work of all the others of the family, or course, to which he belonged. The work went on, from father to son. This was not the case with the prophets. It was not an office they held by inheritance; and besides, the work of one prophet, as it regarded what he had to deliver in the way of revelation, was very different from what it was in another. Moreover, the office of prophet expired with the natural life of him that held it, unless

---

* Heb. i. 1.

others were equally called, by extraordinary circumstances, to sustain it. The office of priest and levite, on the contrary, was held, in common, by a long succession of individuals belonging to the same family, and the same tribe. It was the work, not of a few, but of many; and not confined to particular times, but running through all successive ages, till the work itself, from peculiar circumstances, should terminate.

Connected, however, with ordinary offices, one or two things may here be specified. The first is — They have sometimes been found in conjunction with offices of an extraordinary kind. Thus, Moses, in connexion with his being the inspired legislator of Israel, was found often discharging the ordinary office of a judge. David sustained the ordinary office of king also, with the extraordinary office of prophet. And some of the ordinary priests, such as Jeremiah and Ezekiel, were employed as extraordinary prophets; * and the apostles themselves, coupled the ordinary work of missionaries, agreeably to the commission of their departing Lord, with the extraordinary work of revealing the will of God to men. The former part of their work was, most assuredly, ordinary, being devolved, by our Lord, on others besides them; and thousands, in different ages, have shared with them in it; and there are a goodly number, in our own age, that have traversed a much wider space of either land or sea, owing to modern discoveries, than either were, or could be, traversed by them.

But another circumstance deserving of notice, respecting *ordinary* offices, is — they have, sometimes, been performed by *extraordinary assistance,* and under *extraordinary circumstances.* An instance of this we have in the case of Bezaleel, in preparing the tabernacle, in the wilderness. The spirit of the Lord, we are told, was given him, that he might be filled with wisdom, and un-

---

* Jeremiah i. 1, and Ezekiel i. 3.

G 3

derstanding, and knowledge, in all manner of workmanship. To devise cunning work, to work in gold, and in silver, and in brass, and in cutting of stones, to set them, and in carving of timber, to work in all manner of workmanship. * Aholiab was also given him as a companion. It is evident that the work here spoken of, though for an extraordinary and hallowed purpose, was yet ordinary work. Many, since that day, in various parts of the world, have performed work of this kind. They have wrought, and that most exquisitely, all kinds of work, relating to gold, and silver, and brass, and wood, and stone. The ancients, with Phidias at their head, are proofs of this. Many a famous name, also, in modern times, shews that the work of Bezaleel, and his companion Aholiab, in the wilderness, was work, not uncommon, but shared, with many others, in different ages.

But we remark, farther, that though this work was *ordinary, in itself considered,* it was yet *accomplished by extraordinary assistance.* These men were filled with the spirit of God, for the distinct purpose, of fitting them for their work. Here, then, was ordinary work, to be performed by extraordinary endowment. In addition, this work was performed, thus extraordinarily, by these individuals, *under very extraordinary circumstances.* These were, first, their *call* was immediately from God. Secondly, they wrought under the *eye* and by the *direction of Moses;* for the command to him, relative to every thing connected with the tabernacle, was, that it should be made *according to the pattern* shewn him on the mount : † and, finally, this extraordinary endowment was the result of the necessity of the case. The children of Israel, in any age, were never famous for possessing a taste for the fine arts. How much more, then, might this be supposed to be the case, in the rude age we are now contemplating; even though they had

---

* Exodus xxxi 1-6.   † Exodus xxv. 40, and xxvi. 30.

lately come from the cradle of the sciences, Egypt itself. They were also in a waste howling wilderness, far from the reach of towns, or cities, in which might be found workmen, sufficiently skilled in the various kinds of work that were wanted. When the temple at Jerusalem was reared by Solomon, it was so, not by the use of extraordinary qualifications, as was the case with the tabernacle in the wilderness. No, he had only to send to Tyre, and there he found Hiram, perfectly qualified, in an ordinary way, for rearing his magnificent temple, in all its glory and beauty. * God never gives extraordinary supply, when ordinary can be obtained. It could not be so in the wilderness; and as He had in that wilderness, in the absence of an ordinary supply of food, given them an extraordinary supply, in the bestowment of the manna; and, in addition, as raiment in the wilderness, was not easily procured, He had prevented theirs from waxing old, while they continued in it. In like manner, He endowed the men, above alluded to, extraordinarily, for the work they had to perform, in rearing a tabernacle, in the same wilderness, for his own worship.

Having made these preliminary remarks, we now come to consider their bearing on the point in question—the durability of the evangelists' office. And here, we notice, in the first place, "that there is nothing in the *work* that the evangelists were called to discharge, to prevent that durability. What was that work? Was it not, in reality, missionary work? Is not this generally confessed? Do not modern missionaries perform, substantially, all that they did? Is not the business of a missionary to preach the gospel to the world, either at home or abroad? Is not the conversion of sinners his particular object? Does he not endeavour, when he is rendered the instrument of converting sinners, to unite them in the bonds of

---

* 1 Kings vii. 13, 14.

Christian fellowship? Does he not either become himself their pastor, or help them to look out for one, either from among themselves, or, from some quarter, where a suitable one may likely be found? Does he not assist at the ordination of a pastor among them, if he conceive he is one of the right kind? In short, does he not take a deep interest in their welfare, ever after he has been useful to them? And does he not visit them, with a view to encourage and strengthen them, as often afterward, as he has opportunity? All this we find modern missionaries doing; and, in doing so, they are never supposed to do wrong. They are never complained of, as intruding upon an extraordinary office, that had long since ceased. Well, then, if the work of a modern missionary so exactly corresponds to that of the ancient evangelist, who will deny that the work of the evangelists was ordinary work, like that of Bezaleel and Aholiab? — that is, it was work adapted to every age; and was, therefore, designed to be continued, as well as that of the pastoral office, through every successive generation of man.

But though it may be conceded that the work of the modern missionary resembles that of the ancient evangelist, it may still be objected, that the *call* to that work, the *assistance* obtained in it, and the *manner* of performing it, were very different, in the one case, from what they were in the other. Let us briefly glance at each of these objections. As to the *call* of the evangelists, it was, indeed, extraordinary, in some instances. This was the case with Timothy, respecting whom it is said, that he received his gift by prophecy; but, in connexion with this, it may be stated — that it has sometimes been the case, that an extraordinary call has been given to perform ordinary work. This we have seen was the case with Bezaleel and Aholiab, — their work was ordinary, though their call was extraordinary. So was it, doubtless, with Timothy. Although he had his gift communicated to him, in consequence of the prophecies which went before, concerning him, his work, nevertheless, was ordinary work, the work of a missionary. Besides, *his* extraordinary call does not intimate, that *this* was the case with all the other evangelists. Philip was an evangelist, as well as he, but we hear of no prophecies concerning him. He was chosen to the office of deacon, however; in consequence of his being a man of honest report, and full of the Holy Ghost, and wisdom. This was sufficient, doubtless, to warrant him to engage in the work of evangelizing, when driven by persecution from his station in Jerusalem. In short, every one, on whom the ascended Redeemer conferred the gift of an evangelist, had a sufficient warrant to evangelize; even though no prophecies had gone before, respecting him, and though he never had any extraordinary call to his work. This was sufficient warrant for Paul and Barnabas to take John, surnamed Mark, with them, though not named by the Holy Ghost, when called themselves; and this was sufficient warrant for him to go. In short, every wise man, in whose heart the Lord had put wisdom, ability, and inclination to work, in that age, was called to work in rearing a spiritual temple for God; as well as the wise hearted men among the Israelites, were called to assist in rearing the tabernacle in the wilderness. And who has rescinded this law? Are not all the wise hearted, whom God has enabled to work, and inclined to work, as much called to work, now, as ever, even though no extraordinary call, either by name, or, by prophecy, be given them? But it is not to be forgotten here, that if an extraordinary call is to prove the temporary character of an office, this is as applicable to the *pastoral office, as to the one in question.* The bishops at Ephesus, are said to have been appointed, as such, by the *Holy Ghost.* He who separated Paul and Barnabas to their work, separated also these, for the particular work they were called to. A prophetic intimation, in both cases, was, in all probability, employed; and this was the case, also, with Timothy. If the extraordinary call, then, of Timothy, is a reason for preventing him having successors in his office, it is an equally valid reason why it should prevent the elders of Ephesus having successors in theirs. The fact is, the work of both classes, like that of Bezaleel and Aholiab, was ordinary work, adapted to all times and places; but like theirs, the call of some, at least, of both classes, was extraordinary, in consequence of the peculiar exigences of the church, at that period.

But the same argument is equally applicable to the extraordinary *assistance* the evangelists had, in performing their work. Part of their qualifications were, indeed, extraordinary. They possessed the gift of the word of knowledge, and they wrought miracles, as well as spoke with tongues. It is not to be forgotten, as already intimated, however, that these were bestowed under peculiar circumstances. The necessity of the times, and the circumstances of the Christian religion, called for them. We have seen that, in a case of emergency, an ordinary work may be performed by extraordinary endowment. Such was the case, in the wilderness, with the parties before alluded to — Bezaleel and Aholiab. The remoteness of the situation in which the Israelites then were, together with the circumstance that they themselves were ignorant of the arts, required a special interference, on the part of the Divine Being, in order to the rearing of a tabernacle, to send extraordinary help. Such was the case in the morning of the Christian religion. The religion itself had to be proved as having come from God. The gift of miracles was, accordingly, given to its ministers as the credentials of God's ambassadors. The scriptures, also, were not completed; and, therefore, an extraordinary endowment to instruct, and keep from error, was absolutely necessary. The gift of the word of knowledge, for this end, was, therefore, conferred on the class of officers we are now contemplating; and this gift was of the utmost consequence, as without it, they neither could easily comprehend, nor readily recollect, the Christian doctrine, they had learned from the apostles. Such were the exigences which called for these extraordinary endowments. It was not, therefore, the work, but the circumstances under which it was exercised, which rendered these gifts necessary. The church was then, as it were, in the wilderness, and needed to be fed with manna; but so soon as the wilderness was left — so soon as it obtained a firm footing in the world — the manna was withdrawn, and the produce of Canaan, — the sacred scriptures, — was quite sufficient for all that was needed. This may be affirmed of all the extraordinary endowments of that period. The word of wisdom, and the word of knowledge, together with the gift of prophecy, were all to vanish away. Some of the offices, too, supplied by these gifts, were to vanish away likewise. * This was the case with the apostolic and prophetic offices, as their endowments and work were peculiar and temporary; but as the pastoral work. the building up of the converted, was an every day work, consequently, it survived. In the apostolic age, those who held this office, had not only an extraordinary *call* to it, but they were also extraordinarily *endowed :* they healed the sick, as well as prayed with them, anointing them with oil in the name of the Lord. † They appear, also, to have been endowed with the word of knowledge, as we have seen by comparing Eph. iv. 11, with 1 Cor. xii. 28, 29, where the term "teachers," in the latter passage, seems to answer to the terms evangelist, pastor, and teacher, in the former, As the pastoral office was, then, thus extraordinarily endowed, and yet was an ordinary and permanent office, why should this not be the case with the office of evangelist. If the possession of an extraordinary call and gift, is evidence of an extraordinary office, and, consequently, a tempo-

---

* 1 Cor. xiii. 8.   † James v. 14, 15.

rary one, in the one case, it must be so, equally, in the other. The permanency of the pastoral and the evangelist's office, must, consequently, stand or fall together.

With regard to the *manner* in which the evangelists performed their work, that is another circumstance, raised, as an objection, to their office being continued. They were, it is said, under the guidance and direction of the apostles, and had an authority and power in all the churches, nearly equal to theirs. There is a kind of magic influence in some words, when introduced into certain connections, without allowing ourselves to reflect on their meaning. Such is the case with the terms *power*, and *authority*, in the connexion stated above: — the evangelists had nearly as much power and authority as the apostles. But what power had even the apostles? None, in themselves considered. All their power consisted in the revelation with which they were entrusted. In this respect, they were on a level with Moses, in building the tabernacle. In that matter all the power or authority he had, was to exhibit the pattern God had shewn him in the mount. To that pattern, he had no power to add, or diminish. Bezaleel and Aholiab stood in nearly the same relation to him, in building the earthly tabernacle, that the evangelists stood in to the apostles, in rearing a spiritual temple for God. In the formation of the tabernacle, the inspired artist might tell others what to do, as he himself was directed by Moses; but as Moses himself had no power or authority, to invent, to alter, or to amend; so neither had he. In the rearing of the spiritual temple, it was the same. The apostles were to teach " all things, whatsoever Christ had commanded," and all the doctrines, and duties, and ordinances, of Christianity, were to be an exact counterpart of what they had seen, or heard, or had had revealed to them; as all these were to be attended to, " *as* they had received them," and the ordinances were to be kept "*as* they were delivered." In consequence, there was little room for power here. Legislative authority, in themselves considered, they had none; and their assistants in the missionary work, could have none either. The apostolic rod might, occasionally, be used by the apostles, but this was a power which they could not delegate to another, any more than the spirit of revelation with which they were gifted. The evangelists, therefore, could not use it, any more than they could *reveal* the will of God. As the messengers of God's special ambassadors, however, carrying the verbal mandates of revelation, they had authority to enjoin these; but this is no more than what was attached to the work of the pastors of that day; and, in substance, actually attaches to every faithful minister of Christ, who delivers the commands of his Lord, in the scriptures, to his fellow-creatures. Besides, as we have seen, no power, in ordination, attaches to them, beyond a refusal to ordain those not properly qualified. The primitive presbytery had the same power, and acted on the same principle. So, also, does the modern missionary.

On the whole, then, there appears nothing in the work of the evangelists; in their call to that work; in their qualifications for it; or, in the manner in which they discharged its duties, that is in any way inimical to the office they held being a permanent one; as all that may be urged as objections to its perpetuity, may be equally urged against the permanence of the office of a bishop. The work of the one, is as durable in its nature, as the work of the other. The call and qualifications of the primitive bishops were similar to those of the evangelists; and both of them performed their work, under the eye, and special superintendence, of the apostles, in the absence of their writings. The natural conclusion, then, seems to be, that the one office, as connected with His cause in the world, was designed by God, to be as permanent as the other. But this conclusion, founded on this negative view of the subject, will, we apprehend, be considerably

H

strengthened, when we take into account a number of other circumstances, which appear almost to amount to positive intimations, that it is the will of our Lord, that the office of evangelist should be continued, in his church, to the end of time. These circumstances will come under our review in the ensuing section.

SECTION FOURTH.

The scriptures present several important considerations, which seem to intimate, that it was the intention of the Great Head of the church, that the evangelist's office should be permanent.

The first of these considerations is the calling and sending forth of the seventy by our Lord. These seventy were preachers of the gospel. They were, as such, to say to those to whom they came : " The *kingdom of God* is come nigh unto you." * This was the very work of an *evangelist.* They were, also, like the evangelists, *itinerant preachers ;* they went from place to place, into every city and village, whither our Lord himself intended to come. To these places they went two and two, in company. They were sent out thus, not only to prepare the way for our Lord, as it should seem, but, to assist the twelve apostles, either in the way of relieving them from journeying at this time, as they had been out by themselves some time before, or else to make the present journey less laborious to them. Be this, however, as it might, they were, doubtless, employed as the assistants of the apostles; and as they were sent out, but a short time before our Lord's crucifixion, it seems a likely circumstance, that he intended them to be employed, along with the apostles, in the great work

---

* Luke x. 1-11.

of converting the world, after his resurrection and ascension to glory. The itinerating of the apostles, in the land of Judea, was only preparatory to the greater work of itinerating throughout the world. If help was needed in the one case, by them, much more was it needed in the other. It is the part of a skilful general, before he leads his troops into the field of battle, not only to have them all sufficiently disciplined, but to have them in sufficient numbers. In every army, there is, usually, a reserve of combatants, that when the ranks in the van are thinned, by the fury of the mortal strife, others may be ready instantly to fill up their place. Such an idea seems to have guided the great captain of salvation, in preparing his army for battle. The twelve, he knew, would have to bear the brunt of the fight, and therefore he gave them companions, who would not only assist them in the conflict, but who would be able to catch the standard, when they fell. The names of none of the seventy are mentioned; at least as belonging to that class of labourers. They were, however, all disciples, and truly good men; hence our Lord called on them to "rejoice not only that the devils were subject to them, through his name, but that their names were written in heaven." They were fit men, then, not only for assisting, but for succeeding, the disciples, in their missionary labour. These labours were not only extensive, but undying. The words our Lord were emphatic and remarkable, when he sent out both the twelve and the seventy. "The harvest truly is plenteous, but the labourers are few: pray ye, therefore, the Lord of the harvest, that he would thrust forth more labourers into his harvest." This, however, was true, not only when he sent them out, but when their work on earth was done. It was then as necessary as ever, from the plenteousness of the harvest, to pray to the Lord of the harvest, to thrust into it more labourers. The prayer that our Lord taught *then*, he, doubtless, therefore, wished to be continued.

A similar class of labourers the world ever needed — a similar class of labourers must, therefore, ever have been intended to be employed ; and, therefore, in order to their being raised up, and qualified for their work, it is the duty of the church, in all successive ages, to pray for them ; and, not only to *pray* for them, but to *try* to *find them out*, and *call them forth*, and *support them*, in gathering in the harvest.

Another circumstance, very similar to this, is that of the apostles fixing upon the evangelists, as assistants in this work after our Lord had endowed them for the purpose.   There is no doubt but that all the apostles would have their ministers and fellow-labourers.   To whatever part of the world, from the centre where they diverged, they were to direct their labours, these their assistants, would, doubtless, accompany them. Their number, and names, and places of labour, are now a secret to us.   The Spirit of God has not seen fit to reveal them.   The history of all, however, is known to Him, and to the redeemed congregated in heaven.   All the apostles are there.   The fruits of their labours, their joy and crown of rejoicing, are there, and their assistants also : and all who are, ultimately, conducted to that world, will, consequently, read many a page of history, to which they have no access, at present.   "What we know not now, we shall know, hereafter :" not merely relative to the providence of God towards ourselves, but also, in relation to others.   With the companions of Peter and Paul, we are best acquainted.   The sacred record contains most of their history.   As to the former, we are told that *six brethren* went from Joppa, to the house of Cornelius, along with him.   In the epistles that he wrote to the disciples, in different parts of Asia Minor, he refers to one fellow-labourer of the name of Silvanus, and another of the name of Marcus. As to Paul, his companions are better known, as the narrative of his eventful labours is more full, than that of any other of the eminent labourers of that day.   The names of Barnabas, and John, surnamed Mark, and Silas, and Timothy, and Aquila, and Apollos, and Aristarchus and Alexander, Trophimus and Tychicus, Demas, Artemas and Zenas, together with Onesiphorus, Clement, Cressens and Sosthenes, are familiar to every reader. Doubtless, a number of others, whose names we have never heard of, often assisted him, during his important labours, in different places, in the course of the ever memorable thirty years of his Christian career ; — a career, the singular and glorious events of which, eternity alone can unfold.

Now, all these individuals were engaged along with him and with others, sustaining the same office, for a specific purpose. That, doubtless, was to assist them in their present labours, that thereby they might be put into a suitable course of moral training, and by that training, be fitted to fill their place, as missionaries, when they were gone. Our Lord had acted upon this principle, with respect to the apostles themselves. He was solicitous that all the great truths of Christianity should be distinctly understood by them. In consequence, while he spake in parables only to others, he gave them to know the mysteries of the kingdom. He was ever anxious to get them to drink into his own missionary spirit, exhibited in the way of "going about doing good:" hence, when they came to him at the well of Sychar, and prayed him to eat, "I have meat to eat," said he, "that ye know not of." "My meat is to do the will of him that sent me, and to finish his work." In order to lead their minds to the same work, he took them always with him. And in all their peregrinations along with him, through the Holy Land, he was constantly presenting the future to their view, and reminding them of the glorious triumphs of his kingdom. On one occasion, when comparing himself to a shepherd, and his people to sheep, he says, in allusion to the future ingathering of the Gentiles — "other sheep I have, which are not of this (the Jewish) fold : them also, I must bring, that they may hear my voice; and there shall be one fold, and one shepherd." * In like manner, when it was told him, that certain Greeks were desirous of seeing him, the intelligence appears to have affected him deeply——a circumstance which could not but be observed by his disciples, and must, afterwards, have powerfully operated on their minds. "The hour is come, that the son of man shall be glorified, verily, verily, I say unto you, except a corn of wheat fall into the ground and die, it abideth alone: but if it die, it bringeth forth much fruit. And I, if I be lifted up from the earth, will draw all men unto me." † On another occasion, in adverting to his miraculous works, and what they would be able to do when he had left them, he said to his disciples, "verily, verily, I say unto you, he that believeth in me, the works that I do shall he do also; and greater works than these shall he do; because I go to my father." ‡ He constantly reminded them, too, of the sufferings they should have to endure, and the perils they should have to encounter, in his cause. "The time cometh," he says, "that whosoever killeth you will think that he doeth God service." "In the world ye shall have tribulation, but in me ye shall have peace."‖

Now it must be obvious that all this was moral training; and that all was adapted to fit the individuals concerned,—for the arduous service, in which, in future, they were to be employed. Such, doubtless, was the course which the apostles, afterwards, adopted with regard to the evangelists. They knew that they themselves could not live always; and, as "the prudent man forseeth the evil and hideth himself," so they, doubtless, endeavoured to train others to the work they must leave behind them. They had heard their Lord and Master inculcate the importance of suitable forethought,

* John x. 16.   † John xii. 20-25.   ‡ John xiv. 12.
‖ John xvi. 2, 33.

in the case of the unjust steward. They had heard him
intimate that it was too common, for "the children of
this world to be more wise in their generation, than
the children of light." They had heard him exhort
them to " make to themselves friends of the mammon of
unrighteousness, that when they failed, they might be
received into everlasting habitations." All this could
not have been forgotten by them, and especially now
that the Spirit had taught them all things, and had
brought all things to their remembrance. They knew
that his commission was an undying one. They knew
that they themselves must die, but it must live. Christ
would still have lambs and sheep to be fed, when Peter
had put off his tabernacle, even as the Lord Jesus
Christ had shewed him. It was, therefore, necessary
that Peter should look beyond his own service in this
world, and prepare others to take up that service, when
he should be called to leave it. We have no epistle of
Peter to Mark, as we have of Paul to Timothy. The
Bible, as a portable and generally useful volume, could
not contain all that might be written ; and indeed it
was not neccessary, as what was said to one, was
equally suited to all. In the epistles to Timothy, we
see how intent the apostle was on having his beloved
son in the gospel fitted for the missionary work, before
he left him. " Thou, therefore, my son, be strong in the
grace that is in Christ Jesus." "Thou, therefore, endure hardness, as a good soldier of Jesus Christ. Consider what I say ; and the Lord give thee understanding in all things. Remember that Jesus Christ of the
seed of David was raised from the dead according to
my gospel. Study to shew thyself approved unto God,
a workman that needeth not to be ashamed, rightly
dividing the word of truth. Flee also youthful lusts ;
but follow righteousness, faith, charity, peace, with
them that call on the Lord out of a pure heart. 2 Tim.
ii. throughout. Finally, as he calls on Timothy, to
commit to faithful men, that which had been originally

committed to himself, that they might also teach others; so he himself would act on the same principle to Timothy and others. He would teach them, that, after his decease, they might not only have these things in remembrance, but also teach others. The other apostles, doubtless, would do the same.

Another circumstance that seems to intimate the perpetuity of the evangelist's office, is, the proportion of scripture allotted, by way of direction, to those who sustained that office. The extent of revelation, is ever found to be in proportion to the importance and utility of the matter spoken of. A large portion of the scriptures, both of the Old and New Testaments, consists of history. The reason is, that almost all the didactic parts of the sacred volume are based on the facts that the sacred historians record. Take, for instance, the New Testament, and we shall find, that all that is stated in the epistles, as doctrine, has respect to what is affirmed by the evangelists, relative to the events of our Lord's life, death, and resurrection. The sum, too, of all the duties enjoined, is contained in the holy example which these events exhibit. Let us apply this, then, to the matter in hand. The commission of Christ involves attention to two distinct moral classes of men — the converted, and the unconverted. — The latter, are to have the gospel preached to them ; and the former, are not only to live on the gospel they have already believed, but they are to be taught " all things whatsoever Christ has commanded." This latter duty, we find the New Testament devolving on the *pastors* of the churches, who are called to feed the flock, over which they were made overseers. Here, then, there is an important office, and important duties are assigned to it. Certain qualifications are specified as being necessary, on the part of those who hold that office ; and they themselves, are, here and there, incidentally addressed, relative to their duties, in the sacred pages. All the matter, however, of these addresses is but small and scanty, compared with what is said to evangelists. Three whole epistles are addressed to these. It is remarkable, too, that there is nonothing of an extraordinary nature, referred to in these epistles, relating to the *work* of those addressed. This is truly the case with the epistle to Titus. He is called upon to do nothing but what may be done, and is done, by any ordinary modern missionary. Every modern missionary, with the Bible in his hand, can speak with as much authority as he could. Titus had no authority but what revelation gave him. Every modern missionary can call on the newly formed churches to choose pastors, &c., and can officiate, at their ordination, as well as he could. The same, in substance, may be affirmed of the epistles to Timothy. It is true, he is spoken of as having a "*gift;*" but that gift is not alluded to, as being one of the highest order — it was not the gift of revelation, included in the word of wisdom — it was not a gift that required *repression*, like the gift of the prophets: — no, it required stirring up. It was not to be neglected. It required to be cultivated, by the exercise of "reading." Now all this may be affirmed of the modern missionary, whose ordinary gifts may be aided by divine influence, and by the unerring pages of a complete revelation, which Timothy did not possess. The food of Canaan is a full equivalent to him, for the manna that fell in the wilderness, to Timothy.

It is rather a singular and incongruous circumstance, that those who contend for the extraordinary, and, consequently, the temporary character of the evangelist's office, are ever in the habit of applying what is addressed to Timothy and Titus, to modern ministers and missionaries. Dr. Macknight, for instance, in his valuable commentary on the epistles, speaking respecting the epistles to these two evangelists, says, "that taken together, they contain a full account of the qualifications and duties of the ministers of the gospel; and may be regarded, as a complete body of divinely inspired ecclesiastical canons, to be observed, by the Christian clergy, of all communions, to the end of the world.   These epistles, therefore, ought to be read frequently, and with the greatest attention, by those, in every age and country, who hold sacred offices, or who have it in view to obtain them ; not only that they may regulate their conduct, according to the directions contained in them, but by meditating seriously on the solemn charges delivered to all the ministers of the gospel, in the persons of Timothy and Titus, their minds may be strongly impressed with a sense of the importance of their function, and of the obligation which lieth on them to be faithful in discharging every duty belonging to it." *   Similar ideas, also, are often employed, in many, if not all, of our ordination sermons.   Now, is it not strange ? does it not betray great inconsistency, to appropriate the duties of an office, which it is generally supposed has long since ceased, to those who sustain an office confessedly quite distinct ?   There is, certainly, much more congruity in the address of the late celebrated Robert Hall, to Mr. Eustace Carey, on the eve of his going out as a missionary to India.   "I scarcely need recommend to your attention," said he, "the letters of Saint Paul to Timothy and Titus, where the *office* of an *evangelist (for such you must consider your-self) is delineated, with such precision and fidelity. While you peruse his inspired directions, you are entitled to consider yourself as addressed, inasmuch as the spirit, under whose direction they were written, unquestionably intended them for the instruction of all who are in similar circumstances."* †

It has been said, that "the extraordinary call of the evangelist is apparent, in that no rules are any where given, or prescribed, about their choice, or ordination ; no qualification of their persons is expressed, nor any direction given to the church, as to its future proceeding about them, any more than about new, or other a-

---

* See preface to first epistle to Timothy, sec. 4.
† Works, Vol. L., p. 296.

postles." * In reply, it may be said, that when God gave his word to man, He did so on the principle that the being to whom it was sent, was in possession of reason, or common sense. It needed scarcely to be told, in so many words, that no new apostles could be expected. Any person of common sense, must easily perceive, that no such persons could again arise, and hold office in the church. To be a *witness* of the facts on which the doctrines of Christianity rested, was a circumstance absolutely necessary, in order for any one to sustain the office of an apostle. But how could this be in future ages ? To give an *inspired* explanation of these facts, and to *demonstrate* the doctrines based upon them, as the truth of God, was, also, a work peculiar to an apostle. This, however, had been *sufficiently* done, by those originally appointed to that office. Then what need for any more ? Had the term *apostle*, indeed, included nothing more, as applied to the men that bore it, than merely that of *missionary*, then we should have contended fearlessly, from the commission given them, that they must, in the nature of things, have had successors, and have had them too, even though no specific direction had been given respecting them. The eleven apostles had no revelation given them by our Lord, respecting the choice of a successor to Judas ; but their own common sense, together with his original choice of twelve, led them to it ; and what they did, in this way, was approved of God. So, with regard to evangelists. Although no direct law is presented, in so many terms, that they were to succeed the apostles, in their missionary labour; and that an order of men of this discription, should be connected with the church, to the end of time ; yet, if we have, from circumstances, and the nature of things, what is tantamount to all this, this is quite sufficient. As has been already

* See Dr. Owen's Discourse on the Holy Spirit and spiritual gifts, chap. 3, sec. 12.

mentioned, there is no direct law instituted, respecting the permanence of the pastoral office ; yet who doubts of its permanence ? The circumstance of such an office being appointed, in all the churches, together with the nature of the qualifications of those who held it, and the absolute need of such an office, lead us, at once, to see its propriety. In like manner, the genius of Christianity as a specific for a dying world ; the permanency of our Lord's commission ; the circumstance of the wisdom of God always providing means to gain an end ; the locality of the pastoral office ; our Lord's fixing on assistants for his followers, apparently with a view to be their successors ; the apostles themselves doing the same ; and all this, in connection with three whole epistles, in which the character and duties of evangelists are, as missionaries, in preaching the gospel to the world, and planting and watering churches, clearly pointed out ; and that too, with *scarcely* any reference to *anything extraordinary,* as it respected *themselves,* and *nothing* extraordinary, as it regarded their *work ;* — these considerations united lead us, inevitably to conclude, under the guidance of reason and common sense, that the evangelists were to be that class of locomotive officers, that were intended, in all succeeding ages, to carry the commission of Christ into effect.

But there is another circumstance which, we think, will tend to make all this appear more distinctly still ; and that is the fact of Paul's actually calling on Timothy to be his successor in the missionary field, when the prospect of death was fully before him. " I charge thee before God," says he, "and the Lord Jesus Christ, who shall Judge the quick and the dead, at his appearing and kingdom, *preach the word ;* be instant in season and out of season, reprove, rebuke, exhort, with all long suffering and doctrine. For the time *will come* when they will not endure sound doctrine ; but, after their own lusts, shall they heap to themselves teachers, having itching ears ; and they shall turn away their ears from the truth, and shall be turned unto fables." "But," he adds, "watch thou in all things, endure afflictions, *do the work of an evangelist*, make full proof of thy ministry." Now mark what follows, as a reason why Timothy should do all this; "For," says he, "*I* am *now* ready to be offered up, and the time *of my departure is at hand*," * &c. "I am done," or nearly so, as if he had said, "with working in the way of preaching the gospel, planting churches, and opposing error; but the work itself is not done; it must still be in progress, when I am laid in the grave. It is needful, therefore, my dear Timothy, that thou now exert thyself, by the grace that is in Christ Jesus, to take it up; not, indeed, as an *apostle*, but as an *evangelist*: not as a *revealer* of Christianity, but a *preacher* of it to the world." Paul had, doubtless, as we have seen, trained Timothy for this day by having him almost constantly with him, and by the letter he had previously written to him; and of this he reminds him a little before. "Thou hast fully know my doctrine, manner of life, purpose, faith, long suffering, charity, patience, persecutions, afflictions, which came upon me at Antioch, at Iconium, at Lystra — but out of them all the Lord delivered me: continue thou, then, in the things that thou hast *learned*, and hast been assured of, *knowing of whom thou hast* LEARNED *them*." † That day was, however, now come, and along with it, had come all that trembling anxiety for the future prosperity of the cause of God, which might, naturally be supposed, in the near prospect of death, to fill the mind of him who, in the days of his highest vigour, was in the habit of saying, "Besides those things that are without, that which cometh upon me daily, the care of all the churches."

In this touching portion of the history of these two excellent men, these two dear and ardent friends, we

---

* 2 Tim. iv. 1-6   † 2 Tim. iii. 10-14.

I

are forcibly reminded of some other facts, of a somewhat similar description, mentioned in the sacred record. We are induced, for instance, to cast our eyes backward on the scene exhibited when Joseph, on his dying bed, addressed his brethren. "I die," said he, "and God shall surely visit you, and bring you out of this land, unto the land which he sware to Abraham, to Isaac, and Jacob." "And Joseph," it is farther said, "took an oath of the children of Israel, saying, "God will surely visit you, and ye shall carry my bones from hence." * Here, then, on a dying bed, was ardent faith, in the certainty of the continuance of the cause of God; and an earnest call, at the same time, to those left behind, to do their duty, in carrying it on. We are also forcibly reminded of the charge of Moses to Joshua. "Be strong," said he to him, "and of a good courage; for thou shalt bring the children of Israel into the land that I swear unto them; and I will be with thee." † Here we perceive, that Joshua was called to be the *successor* of *Moses*, not as the *legislator*, but as the *leader*, of Israel; just as *Timothy*, at the time referred to above, was called to be the *successor* of Paul, not as a *revealer*, but as a *proclaimer*, of the *gospel*. Finally, we are reminded of the valedictory address of Paul himself, at a former period, to the elders of Ephesus. "Take heed therefore unto yourselves, and to all the flock,—to feed the church of God, which he hath purchased with his own blood. For I know this, that after my departing, shall grievous wolves enter in among you, not sparing the flock. Therefore watch, and remember, that by the space of three years, I ceased not to warn every one, night and day, with tears. And now, brethren, I commend you to God, and to the word of his Grace," &c. "I have coveted no man's silver, or gold," &c. "I have shewed you all

---

* Gen. 50. 24, 25.   † Deut. xxxi. 23.

things, how that so labouring ye ought to support the weak," &c.* Comparing this address, with that to Timothy, we perceive a considerable similarity, mingled with a strong shade of contrast. The elders, as overseers and pastors, are called upon to feed the flock; and Timothy, as an evangelist, is called upon to preach the gospel. This circumstance, then, compared with others stated in the New Testament, and to some of which we have already referred, would seem to intimate, that it was the intention of our Lord, that the separate parts of his commission, the one referring to the world, and the other to the church, should devolve, finally, on two distinct classes of officers; the one, the evangelists, to preach the glad tidings of mercy to a lost and guilty world; and the other, the pastors, to build up believers on their most holy faith.

The last circumstance we shall mention, as showing that it was the design of the head of the church, that a class of missionary labourers should be continued in all successive ages, is, — The call given to Timothy, that he should look out for other men to succeed himself. Hence says Paul, " The things that thou hast heard of me, among many witnesses, the same commit thou to faithful men, who shall be able to teach others also." † In this declaration, the following things are worthy of notice. First, Paul intimates, that at a previous period, Timothy had heard certain things, uttered by him, and had had these things, at that time, committed to him. In this, in all likelihood, he alludes to the charge he gave him, when he ordained him to be an evangelist, in conjunction with the presbytery of Lystra and Iconium, who were, probably, along with others, the many witnesses here referred to, among whom the charge was delivered. Secondly, this same charge, Timothy was to commit to others who were faithful men. The

---

* Acts xx. 28-35.   † 2 Tim. ii. 2.

word of the truth of the gospel had been given in charge
to himself, as a faithful man, in order to preach it to every
creature.   Well! the same truth was to be committed by
him to others, doubtless, to do the same work, as the
same work was as needful to be done *afterwards*, as
when first committed to him.   Thirdly, This work was to
be devolved on these faithful men, that they might teach
" others also."   Now, " the others" the apostle here alludes to, were, undoubtedly, persons that Timothy would
not have an opportunity of teaching; and this owing, more
to the circumstance of their living beyond the limits of his
mortal life, than their being, from their present geogra-
phical position, beyond the range of his evangelical
labours.

It has, however, been generally thought, that the
faithful men, here referred to, were the pastors of the
churches that Timothy was called upon to ordain.
To this it may be replied, that there can be no doubt,
that when bishops were ordained, they had committed to them — the truth of God, in order that they
might feed the flock over which they had been placed as
overseers ; but what evidence have we, that these are,
in the passage under consideration, specially alluded to ?
Were other labourers not needed, as well as they ?
Were missionaries no longer to be employed, in order to
the conversion of the world ?   Was the commission of
Christ to close when the work of Timothy, as an evangelist, was over ?   Assuredly not.   Then why may not
evangelists be referred to here, as well as bishops ?
Should we allow that bishops are, indeed, here spoken
of, is there any sufficient reason to show, that they a-
lone are referred to ?   We think not.   Besides, it really
seems more probable that evangelists are here chiefly
alluded to.   One reason is, the office of bishop is not
referred to, in all this epistle.   The apostle is not speaking of bishops.   Had the passage occurred in the first
epistle, we should have been led, very naturally, to suppose that, to these, and these alone, he was alluding ;

but this is not the case; therefore, it is not likely that bishops are hinted at, by the apostle, here. Another reason is, — the evangelist's work is particularly alluded to, in other parts of the letter. Paul alludes to a number of evangelists by name, in the last chapter; and, as we have seen, calls on Timothy to do the work of an evangelist; and all the directions he gives him, in the epistle, have particular regard to his work, as an evangelist. Such being the case, then, it seems more natural to conclude, that evangelists are here alluded to, than pastors. Lastly, Paul, with the utmost seriousness, in the prospect of his own death, calls on Timothy, the more diligently to attend to the work in which, as missionaries, they had been jointly engaged; as Timothy, also, was mortal, as well as himself; and as the work itself was not to die with Timothy, it rather seems natural to suppose, that Paul, in the letter in which he so touchingly refers to his own death, should hint, likewise, at Timothy's, and call on him to give in charge to others, as his successors in the same work, that important truth, which had been, at a previous time, and was now, again, so solemnly, committed to himself.

All these circumstances, then, in combination, make it appear somewhat evident, to say the least of it, that the great head of the church intended the evangelists to succeed the apostles, in their missionary labour; and, also, that other missionaries, in all successive ages, should arise to succeed them. It is still, however, frankly confessed, that nothing positive is said, — no direct command is given respecting the permanence of the office; but, as has been noticed, this may also be affirmed respecting the pastoral office. *Its* permanence is, however, allowed, — and allowed from inference. Surely, then, if the inferences for the permanence of the one office, be equally numerous and equally fair, with those for the permanence of the other, every candid mind must inevitably conclude, that the one office must be as permanent as the other.

SECTION FIFTH.

The office was actually continued, after the apostolic age, in the second and third centuries, as the missionaries, at that period, were termed evangelists.

The words of Eusebius are very clear on this head. "There were many," he says, "that flourished at that time, who obtained the first step of apostolic succession, and builded the churches, every where planted by the a- postles. By preaching and sowing the celestial seed of the kingdom of heaven, throughout the world, they filled the garners of God with increase. For the greater part of the disciples then living, affected with great zeal for the word of God, in the first place fulfilled the heavenly commandment, by distributing their substance to the poor. After this, they itinerated ; thereby fulfilling the work and office of evangelists : that is, they preached Christ unto those who, as yet, had not heard of the doc- trine of faith, and published earnestly the doctrine of the holy gospel. These men having planted the gospel in various new and strange places, ordained other pastors, committing unto them the tillage of the new ground, and the oversight of such as were lately converted to the faith ; passing away themselves unto other people and countries. It is impossible, however, to mention by name, all those who were pastors and evangelists, in the first succession of the apostles, in the churches scattered throughout the world." * Such are the declarations of Eusebius on the subject ; and no terms could convey a more just idea of what appears to be the design of the evangelist's office. The evangelists were ambulatory,

---

* Ecclesiastical History, Book III. Chap. 33.

not stationary, preachers. They were not pastors, but they prepared the way for them. They were numerous, and had been rendered very successful, in different parts of the world. Finally, they were still called evangelists. None of the names of these evangelists are stated, but those of Clemens, Ignatius, Polycarp, and Quadratus. It is not improbable that these were evangelists originally; though they became bishops afterwards.

Such, then, was the state of the case, in the early part of the second century; and we find it was the same at its close. At that time, we are told, by the same authority, that a very able scholar, at the head of the catechetical school of Alexandria, of the name of Pantænus, went out as a missionary from that place. The words of Eusebius, respecting him, are as follow: "He is said to have shewed such a willing mind towards the publishing of the doctrine of Christ, that he became a preacher of the gospel unto the eastern gentiles; and was sent as far as India. There were *then, many evangelists* prepared for this purpose, to promote, and plant the heavenly word with godly zeal, after the manner of the apostles. Of these, Pantænus, being one, is said to have gone to India, and to have found there the gospel of Matthew, written in the Hebrew tongue, preserved by those that knew Christ, which, before his coming, had been preached there, by Bartholomew, one of the apostles,"* Here, then, missionaries are again referred to. They are, likewise, spoken of as being many, and very zealous. They are, also, still called evangelists; and they are so, without the least hint of their possessing any extraordinary qualifications. With regard to those spoken of, at the beginning of this century, already referred to, Eusebius makes the following remark, "They wrought miraculously by the power of the Holy Ghost." Be this, however, as it might, nothing of this kind is affirmed respect-

---

* Ecclesiastical History, Book V. Chap. 9.

ing Pantænus and the other evangelists, at the end of the
century.   The Christian canon was then, doubtless, in
the hands of most of the ministers of all descriptions, and,
consequently, there was little or no need of miraculous
supply.   Besides, what may be affirmed by any of the
ecclesiastical historians, or others, respecting miraculous
supply, at this period, is little to be credited.   The necessity for it was now gone by.

Among the evangelists of the second century, may be
included Pothinus and Irenæus. They seem to have been,
originally, members of the church at Smyrna ; and had,
probably, been brought to the knowledge and love of the
truth under Polycarp, the pastor of that church. They appear to have been sent as missionaries, to the cities of Lyons and Vienne, in the south east of France.   The precise
year is not known when the mission was founded ; though
it is probable it may have been between 150 and 160.
They seem to have been, as missionaries, very successful, as two churches, apparently very numerous, were
formed at the above mentioned places.   Pothinus was
the elder of the two, and became the pastor of the
church at Lyons.   He was martyred in his ninetieth
year, and Irenæus succeeded him.   The persecution of
the church at Lyons happened, according to Mosheim,
about the year 177.   A most touching letter, one of the
finest relics of antiquity, was written by the believers in
Lyons and Vienne, to the Asiatic and Phrygian churches,
who are supposed, in conjunction with the church at
Smyrna, to have sent them on their mission. *

In the early part of the third century, we find the
celebrated Origen acting the part not only of a *teacher*,
attached to the church at Alexandria, but of an *evangelist*.   He seems to have travelled to Rome, and Greece,
and Antioch ; in all which places he taught Christianity.
We find that he was sent for, specially, to go to Arabia,

---

* Eusebius', Ecclesiastical History, Book V. Chap. I.

as a missionary, to preach the gospel. Eusebius says respecting him —— "That when he was at Alexandria, there came a certain soldier from the governor of Arabia, with letters to Demetrius, bishop of the see of Alexandria, and to the governor of Egypt, requesting them, with all speed, to send Origen to him, that he might communicate to him some part of his doctrine. Origen, accordingly, took his journey to Arabia; and when he had accomplished its object, returned again to Alexandria."[*] It was, also, during this century, that a number of missionaries pushed the conquests of Christianity, considerably far to the north of France, and south of Germany. We are not distinctly informed whence they came. It is probable, however, that they came from Lyons and its neighbourhood, or else, might be a new reinforcement of missionaries, from Asia. Their names appears to be of Grecian origin. Hence says Mosheim, on the authority of Gregory of Tours, "Dionysius and Gatian, Trophymus, Paul, Saturninus, Martian, and Strumius, men of exemplary piety, passed into France; and amidst dangers and trials of various kinds, erected churches at Paris, Tours, Arles, and other places. This was followed by a rapid spread of the gospel, as the disciples of these pious teachers diffused, in a short time, the knowledge of Christianity, over the whole country." The German churches of Cologne, Treves, Metz, and other places, were founded by Eucharius, Valerius, Maternus, and Clemens. The Goths, also, in Moesia, and Thrace, on the north of Macedonia, were brought under the influence of Christianity, by certain teachers, sent for the purpose, from Asia.[†]

Such are the names of the principal missionaries, or

---

[*] Ecclesiastical History, Book vi. Chap 19.

[†] Mosheim's Ecclesiastical History, Third Century, Part I. Chap. i. Sec. 7.

evangelists, as Eusebius calls them, in the three first centuries — the golden era of Christianity. It is much to be regreted that our accounts of the manner of spreading the gospel, at that period, and of those who spread it, are so scanty. We have a number of names of bishops, in certain places, but we have but little of their personal history. It is probable some of them, like Pothinus and Irenæus, might, in the first instance, be evangelists, and afterwards settled with the churches they were the means of collecting. Others might be those selected by the newly raised churches, under the auspices of those evangelists, who, as Eusebius tells us, after they had planted churches, and had committed the tillage of the new ground to other pastors, passed away to other people and countries. There can be little doubt that many of the evangelists would be sent out, by the churches they were connected with. The catechists and presbyters, in the different churches, as in the cases of Pantænus and Origen, would have, it is highly probable, this honour frequently conferred upon them. These, in all likelihood, would act the part of local evangelists in the neighbourhoods in which the churches, with which they were connected, were situated ; and would thus be fitted for going to distant countries, to preach the gospel to those who had never before heard of it. Some of these, probably, would be invited to these distant stations, by some Christians, who had been previously there. Many, doubtless, like Lydia, would travel to different and distant lands, in carrying on their employments. In these countries, they would try to convince, in a private way, at least, those who were given to idolatry, that they were wrong. They might do so with some degree of success, and this might in-duce them to apply to the Christian societies they had left, to send missionaries to those places. But while some might do this, in the way of commerce, others might do it in the way of war. Soldiers have been Christians ; and some of them very eminent ones ; as for instance, Cornelius. These have often had to travel through many lands, and in doing so, have often been the means of diffusing the gospel. This has been the case, either through their personal exertions, or by means of inducing missionaries to come and occupy uncultivated fields of labour. There have been many interesting incidents of this kind, in different periods of the history of Christianity; and there is every reason to believe, they would often find their counterparts, in the annals of the first three centuries, had they been preserved to us.

As to the means of the support of the missionaries, at this period, we have no reason to suppose it would be materially, if at all, different from what it was in the first century. The law was still binding, "That they who preach the gospel should live by it;" and as those who travelled, as missionaries, had less opportunity of earning anything, by which they might be supported, it seemed the especial duty of Christians, to maintain them. We see the need of such support in modern times, and, doubtless, there would be equal need at the time contemplated. We are not aware that any particular mention is made of any church, or number of churches, supporting *any* of the *many evangelists*, alluded to by Eusebius; but there seems no doubt, that when churches sent them out, they would, if they needed, supply their wants. The churches at that period, it is certain, made most generous contributions to supply the wants of the poor among themselves; and even of strangers, that came to reside near them, and were unable to support themselves. They also supplied the wants of their brethren, who had, on account of their adherence to the Christian faith, been condemned to mines, to islands, and prisons. This we are told, by Justin and Tertullian, in their apologies. *   Now if

---

* See the first apology of Justin Martyr, Chap. 86, and also the apology of Tertullian, Chap. 39.

they did all this, is it likely that they would let the Christian missionaries want? No,—if they relieved that missionary when he was cast into prison, they would equally support him in his work of spreading the gospel, *provided he needed it, and wished it.* It is highly probable, that those among the evangelists who had property, would support themselves. Such appears to have been the case with Origen; hence Eusebius tells us that he disposed of part, at least, of his library, engaging with the individual who purchased it for a very small sum every day to supply his wants. These wants he contrived to be as few as possible, as he acted literally, upon our Lord's direction of not having two coats, or two pairs of shoes. He also abstained from wine, and lived, in other respects, most abstemiously. When entreated, on occasions, to receive a supply to meet his wants, he would not accept of it, and offended, it is said, many, by so doing.* Every missionary is left to his own discretion in these matters; and happy is he who condemneth not himself in the thing that he alloweth. In the case of the apostle Paul, we find instances in which he would not take support, and other instances in which he did so. There is nothing wrong, then, in either taking, or not taking. Origen did not act wrong, in not receiving the supplies that others were anxious to give him. On the other hand, they who took these supplies, as Paul did, in the case of the Philippians, were only receiving the hire of the labourer, who, as we are repeatedly told by the highest authority, is worthy of his reward.

It is a fact also, asserted by Mosheim, and likewise by Gibbon that the Christian scriptures, together with the Old Testament, were widely diffused, before the end of the third century. This was done, we are told, at the expence of many of the more opulent among the

---

* Ecclesiastical History, Book VI. Chap. 2.

Christians, who generously contributed a great deal of their substance to the carrying on of these pious undertakings. One of the most distinguished of these, was Pamphilus of Cæsarea. Cave, on the authority of Hierocles and Eusebius, affirms that, "among other instances of charity, he used freely and readily to bestow the scriptures upon all who were willing to read them. For which purpose, he had always *great numbers* of those holy volumes *by him*, that, as occasion served, he might distribute them. By these means, he mercifully furnished those persons with those divine treasures, whose purses could not, otherwise, reach to the price of the scriptures; far more expensive in those days, than since printing came into the world." * Dr. Adam Clarke, also, in his " Succession of Sacred Literature," mentions that Isidore of Seville, says that " Pamphilus erected at Cæsarea, a library containing 30,000 volumes; and, that his collection was for the purpose of lending out for the use of religiously disposed people."—"This," says the Doctor, " is, if I mistake not, the first notice we have of a circulating library." †

Now, as all this was done, in order to the circulation of the scriptures, we may be certain that the same spirit that did all this, would lead to the encouragement and support of men, to preach in those places, where, as yet, Christianity was unknown. Such we find to have been the case with Chrysostom, some time after the period we have been surveying. Cave, in his " Primitive Christianity," on the authority of the historian Theodoret, affirms, that " He was so zealous about the conversion of infidels, that he employed a number of presbyters and monks, supported, partly, at his own charge, and, partly, at the charge of certain pious and well disposed persons, to go, as missionaries, and to

* Primitive Christianity, Part III. Chap. ii.
† Succession of Sacred Literature, page 226, first edition.

K

make it their sole business to instruct the heathen, in the principles of the Christian faith."* There is no reason to suppose that the conduct of Chrysostom was original, in what he did, in this matter. In the same spirit of zeal and self-denial, had Christianity, doubtless, been spread in the glorious golden ages which had preceded. There is a passage in the letter of Dionysius the bishop of Corinth, to the church at Rome, which seems almost to intimate, that this had been the case with the Roman community, under the auspices of Soter their bishop. "It has been," says he, "your accustomed manner, from the beginning, in different ways, to benefit all the brethren: to send relief not only to the poor in the city, but, particularly, to the brethren appointed to slavish drudgery and digging of metals." "You Romans," he adds, "of old, do retain the paternal affection of Rome, which holy Soter your bishop, not only observed, but also augmented, ministering large and liberal relief to the use of the saints, embracing lovingly the converted brethren as a father does his sons, with the exhortation of holy doctrine."† We are forcibly reminded, by these expressions, of the words of the apostle in addressing the Hebrews. "God is not unrighteous to forget your work and labour of love, which ye have shewed toward his name, in that ye have ministered to the saints, and do minister."‡ The saints, here alluded to, seem to have been the missionary labourers of these days; and the saints whom Soter and the Roman Christians relieved, taken in connexion with what is said about their conduct to the converted brethren, that is, we think, the brethren newly converted, appear to have been labourers of the same stamp, at a later period; and, in all likelihood,

---

* Primitive Christianity, Part III. Chap. ii.
† Eusebius' Ecclesiastical History, Book IV. Chap. xxii.
‡ Heb. vi. 10.

those very evangelists, whom Eusebius speaks of, as being very numerous at that time. It is exceedingly likely, also, that the Asiatic and Phrygian churches would support Pothinus and Irenæus, as their missionaries in France, until the Christian converts at Lyons were able to support them, or, until, like some missionaries of modern times, they were able to support themselves.

In these various statements, then, relative to the history of Christianity in the second and third centuries, we are led to see, that the office in question existed after the death of the first evangelists. The "faithful men," to whom Timothy had committed the truth of God, entrusted originally to his own care, succeeded to the work, after he was gone, as he, himself, had done, in the case of Paul. We know little of these men. We know not their names; most of them at least; but they are written in the Lamb's book of life. Worldly fame is of little consequence. A place, even in ecclesiastical history, is of little moment, in comparison of our finally meeting with the approbation of the chief shepherd; and receiving from his hand a crown of glory that fadeth not away. "They that be wise," in the true sense of the term, whether remembered in this world or not, "shall shine," at last, "as the brightness of the firmament; and they that turn many to righteousness as the stars for ever and ever." Such, doubtless, will be the eternal reward of the evangelists, who lived at the period we have now been contemplating. It would have been well for the world that such a race of men, and such a class of officers in the Christian church, had continued; or, at least, had continued in the full possession of their spirit. This, however, was not the case. We are not to regard this circumstance, however, as inimical to our position, namely, that the evangelist's office was a permanent one. The office, indeed, henceforward, is found in a state of abeyance; but this arose more from moral causes in the church, than from any scriptural evidence that the office itself should henceforth terminate. It will be our object to shew, in the following section, what these causes were.

SECTION SIXTH.

The state of abeyance into which the office of the genuine evangelist sunk, in the succeeding centuries, till after the reformation, sprang rather from moral causes in the church, than from any conviction that the office itself was to cease.

We have already traced the progress of the cause of missions, in the first three centuries, under the able guidance of the original missionaries, the apostles and evangelists, and also, of those who succeeded them. The period, however, that now opens upon us, is dark and dreary. Through a long vista of years, that dark_ness and dreariness continually appear to increase, until they actually become almost palpable. It was then, indeed, the dark midnight of the dreary winter of Christianity. The longest night, however, has its morning, and that morning, to Christianity, at length, came. The twilight of the evening, however, now claims our attention. After the close of the third century, we find the office of the true missionary greatly in abeyance. The shadow of it, it is true, still continued ; but, generally speaking, the genuine missionary — the pious humble preacher of sal_vation by Christ, is withdrawn from the scene ; and individuals and nations are converted, not by the scrip_tural weapons of the Christian warfare, which had, here_tofore, been mighty, through God, to the pulling down of strongholds ; but by the pious frauds, and fantastic mummeries, of ecclesiastics ; aided by the edicts and ar_mies of monarchs. The character of the mission of Austin, under the auspices of Pope Gregory the great, to our own island, in the latter part of the sixth century,

is proof of this. * This, however, is only a single specimen; but it is one of the most favourable: no blood
was shed, as was the case in numbers of other instances.
In the midst, however, of this spiritual gloom that thus
sat brooding over Christendom, like the darkness over
the primeval chaotic mass, the world was, here and there,
and now and then, in part, irradiated, by certain lights,
emitting a glimmering lustre, in different parts of the
horizon. It is a remarkable circumstance, too, that the
brightest light, at this period, was emitted, by what is
deemed now the darkest spot of the British empire.
Ireland, at that time, according to the testimony of its
historians, was a green oasis, in a spiritual point of
view, in the midst of an extensive arid desert — the e-
merald isle, in more senses than one. † From the sixth,
to the ninth century, it was the retreat of the learning
of Europe. Irish missionaries then converted the bar-
barians of Scotland and England, as well as those of the
Continent, and thus by their exertions at that gloomy
period, kept alive the spark of vital Christianity. The
dissenters, or heretics, as they were reputed, also, during the dark ages, in their secluded situations, retained
much of scriptural light, and endeavoured silently to
diffuse divine truth around them. God, we see, from all
these particulars, even in the darkest ages, " ordained a
lamp for his anointed." Still the office of evangelist became, in a great degree, eclipsed. It was shorn both of
its purity and eminence in the church; and, henceforth,
the name is scarcely ever heard of. Various reasons,
doubtless, contributed to this. These reasons, however,

---

* See Rapin's History of England, Vol. I. page 65. London.
Ed. 1732.

† See the History of Ireland, by Elizabeth Blacket. To those
not possessed of larger works, we would strongly recommend this,
on account of its brevity and cheapness. It is also written in a
pleasing style and an excellent spirit.

do not appear to have arisen from any conviction, either from scripture, or from tradition, that the office was intended to sink ; and, consequently, ought to sink into dissuetude. No: Eusebius, who lived in the end of the third, and early part of the fourth, century, never throws out the least hint that the evangelist's office either had ceased, or was to cease. On the contrary, as he calls the missionary labourers, in the end of the second, and beginning of the third century, evangelists, there appears the clearest possible evidence, that it was the opinion of the Christians of that time, that their office was not a temporary one, but to be continued, in the church, in all succeeding ages. In all the other writers, too, previous to the time of Eusebius, so far as we are aware of, there is also nothing to lead to a contrary conclusion. From whatever cause or causes, then, the eclipse of the office proceeded, it does not appear to have arisen from the conviction that it ought, from either divine authority, or its own nature, to be discontinued.

Still the question recurs, What were the causes which led to its abeyance ? In reply, it may be safely affirmed that, it arose from certain moral causes in the church itself. Moral causes are well known to act powerfully on the views, the feelings, and the conduct of men. They lead some to believe, and others to disbelieve divine revelation. They often make the perceptions of some, keen to good, and those of others, keen to evil. Moral causes, also, often produce a wonderful reaction on the conduct of men : thus the pious man seeks to become increasingly so ; hence it is said, " The righteous shall hold on his way, and he that hath clean hands shall wax stronger and stronger." On the other hand, a vicious man is disposed, from his very viciousness, to be more and more so : hence says the apostle, " Evil men and seducers wax worse and worse, deceiving and being deceived." This idea is illustrated, in the early and succeeding periods of the Christian Church. The more zealous the

Christians of the first three centuries were, the more their zeal increased ; and, on the contrary the more worldly minded they were, in the succeeding centuries, the more worldly minded and spiritually indolent did they become. Here, then, is the true cause of either the disuse, or the improper use, of the missionary's work and office, in the times succeeding those we have already contemplated. It may not be improper, however, here, to enter a little more into detail, respecting some of the more prominent of these causes.

The first of them, then, and the root of all the rest, may be said to have been the decay of piety and zeal, among the great body of the professors of religion. True godliness prevailed in the apostolic age, and hence their missionary zeal and usefulness. This zeal burnt brightly, with greater or lesser intensity, till the middle of the second century ; and a gradual decline, from that period, is perceptible. At the close of the third century, this declension had arrived at a most alarming height. The terms are truly affecting, employed by Eusebius, in describing it.* Now, if such was the case at this time, how much more must it have been afterwards, when many more temptations presented themselves ? The decay of piety and zeal, then, may be regarded as the root of the evil we are now considering, namely, the disuse of the office of evangelist in the church, at least in all its pristine importance and usefulness. Very pertinent are the remarks of the excellent and judicious Mr. Thomas Scott on this subject, in his commentary on the 11th verse of the 4th chapter of the epistle to the Ephesians. In remarking on the term evangelist, he, in the first place, makes a quotation from Beza to the following effect: "Under this name, they are to be understood whom the apostles used as their attendants, in performing their office, be-

---

* Ecclesiastical History, Book VIII. Chap. xxx.

cause they were not sufficient for every thing.   Of this
kind were Timothy, Titus, Silvanus, Apollos, whom
Paul joined with himself, in the inscription of the
epistles ; yet so as to call himself, alone, an apostle.
This office, therefore, was only temporary."   On this
quotation Mr. Scott remarks, "The opinion of this
venerable reformer in the last clause, perhaps, is not well
founded.   The office of evangelist seems to have been,
in most respects, similar to that of missionaries, in
subsequent times.   They were preachers of the gospel,
*without full apostolic authority,** and without any stated
charge, going among the heathen to found churches ;
while the apostles lived, under their personal direction,
and, *afterward,* according to their doctrine and methods
of proceeding ; or visiting the churches already planted,
" to set in order such things as were wanting," to supply
the deficiences, or aid the labours, of stated pastors,
and to stimulate them to greater earnestness in discharging their duties.   *When zeal for propagating the
gospel subsided, this office sunk into disuse,* and thus, for
ages, the heathen have been in a great measure neglected : but in *one form or another,* the *office* of *evangelist,*
or *something of the same nature,* must revive, along with
the spirit of evangelizing the nations."   These remarks
seem exceedingly just, in the main, both as it relates to
the nature of the evangelist's office, and the means of its

---

* The idea of half apostolic authority is indeed ludicrous ; but
the term *full,* in the above connexion, suggests it.   Mr. Macleod's
remark is here well worth insertion.   " It appears to us that some
have greatly exaggerated the nature of this office, and said very ex-
travagant things rsepecting them (the evangelists), as though they
were possessed of delegated apostolic authority, and exercised such
high authority over elders and churches, as the apostles themselves
would have done, had they been present.   Why should I trouble
the reader with a confutation of propositions so entirely extrava-
gant ?   There was no such thing as delegated apostolic authority ;
and, besides, the prophets, who were in all the churches, were superior to evangelists.   *View of Inspiration,* page 483.

disuse. The want of piety, or its low condition, in the church, has been the great cause of the lack of missionary exertion; and wherever, or whenever, a revival of pure and undefiled religion has taken place, there, and then, have Christians been inclined to seek the salvation of mankind. *Personal* and *pecuniary* exertions have then, not only been *spoken of*, but *made*; and home labourers and foreign labourers have been called into the field, having volutarily presented themselves, as willing to spend and to be spent for Christ, and the salvation of the souls of men. In short, the history of the church, in every age, shews the intimate connexion of fervent piety, and the office of evangelist. When the one has revived, the other has revived; and, on the contrary, where the one has declined, the other has, uniformly, declined likewise. The history of the church, in modern times, as well as those we are now contemplating, throws much light on this point.*

But while the decline of piety in the church, was the radical cause of the decline of zeal and missionary exertion; other causes, resulting from it, and partly reacting upon it, were also at work. One of these was, the prevalence in the church, of the spirit of a vain philosophy. Human learning, when properly used, is rather friendly to piety, than otherwise. When, however, it is employed to correct revelation, rather than to illustrate it, it usually proves most pernicious. Succeeding events have proved the soundness of the advice that Paul gave to the Colossians, "Beware lest any man spoil you through philosophy and vain deceit, after the tradition of men, after the rudiments of this world, and not after Christ."† Nothing proved more baneful to Christianity, in the

---

* See Brown's History of the propagation of Christianity; and the History of the Revivals in the British Isles, &c. By the author of the memoir of the Rev. M. Bruen.

† Colossians ii. 8.

early periods of its history, than its incorporation with the Platonic philosophy. The system of Ammonius Saccas, which crept into the church through the ascendancy of the genius of Origen, corrupted the Christian belief at the very core, and paved the way for the union of Christianity and heathenism, that, ere long, followed. The prevailing tenet of the sage, named above, was, that all religions were equally true ; and that, by certain allegorical explanations, both the mythology of heathenism, and the sacred writings of Christianity, might be made to harmonize with the system of philosophy that he taught, and which had descended from the oriental sage Hermes, through the Grecian Plato, to himself, the founder of the new Platonic sect, in the school of Alexandria.* Now, it required no prophetic spirit to foretell what would be the result of such views, operating on the mass of the professors of Christianity. The first great baneful effect was ——the scriptures were reduced to a nonentity. If any wished to settle a controverted point, by taking sure footing on some passage of sacred writ, he instantly found himself aloft in the aerial regions, in consequence of the allegorizing propensity of his opponent. Another equally pernicious result was, that, as all religions were nearly equally true, or, at least, fundamentally so, then, it naturally followed, that little trouble need to be expended on the conversion of the heathen. "Go into all the world and preach the gospel to every creature : he that believeth and is baptized shall be saved, and he that believeth not shall be damned," is a precept that would be but little felt by any mind, the prevailing idea of which was, that all worship was alike acceptable to God. We see the effect of the prevalence of this idea, in our own day, on

---

* See this subject fully treated by Mosheim, in his general history, Cent. 3, Part ii. Chap. 1. ; and also in his commentaries, Vol. II. Page 124, &c.

many who profess to be Christians. By how many of these is the stanza of Pope lauded to the skies.

> "Father of all in every age,
> In every clime adored,
> By saint, by savage, or by sage,
> Jehovah, Jove, or Lord."

The efforts of the Twinings and Scott Warings of our own day, to prevent missionaries going to India, arising from similar views, cannot be speedily forgotten. *

Here, then, was one powerful moral cause, operating at the time we are contemplating. It was introduced into the church, at the end of the second century; but made but little way till embraced, in its leading features, by some of the most celebrated men of the third. At the period we are, however, now considering, it had diffused itself, in a greater or lesser degree, over the wide surface of Christianity; and, afterwards, spread itself still more widely, in consequence of its union with other causes equally deleterious.

One of these was, the incorporation of the Christian church, as the religion of the Roman empire. We do not wish, at present, to enter upon the much controverted point of the union of church and state. We only wish to state the fact, that such union tended very much to set aside the spiritual missionary, from going, in his simple garb, to heathen nations, to tell them the story of love — the good news of mercy to man. A shorter way, for the most part, was henceforward adopted, than either the moral persuasion, or tender entreaties of such a man. The mandates of the monarch, enforced by the swords of his warriors, were either the precursors, or the accompaniments, of the missionary

---

* See Fuller's apology for Christian Missions, &c., and Robert Hall's Address on the renewal of the East India Company's Charter.

now. We must not, therefore, now look for the evangelist of either the first or the second century.

In addition, however, to these, there was another
moral cause, that tended, for a very lengthened period, to retard, the missionary zeal of Christians,
by directing it, almost entirely, into another channel;
and that was the controversies and contentions, that
sprung up among Christians themselves. It was the
saying of our Lord, that "A kingdom divided against
itself cannot stand." His own professed kingdom, however, at this time, was most affectingly divided against
itself. If, therefore, it did not come to complete ruin,
it did not enlarge its boundaries; or, at least, did not
enlarge them in the way it ought to have done. Nothing tends more to deaden piety, or to quench zeal for
the spread of the gospel, than Christians contending
one with another, and, especially, as is too frequently
the case, about matters of pure revelation, which are
far removed from the ken, and consequently from the
the decision, of mortals. How much, for instance, was
the reformation retarded, by the internal disputes of Protestants.* It was the Arian controversy, that nearly
brought Nonconformity to its grave, in the beginning
of the eighteenth century; and actually swamped Pres-
byterianism, and the party of the General Baptists, in
the southern part of the island.† It was the same
controversy that raged, at the period we are now considering, and long after, in the Christian church, sapping
almost all its godliness, and blunting all its zeal. Milner,
in his history, makes the following remarks respecting
its effects. Speaking of the extension of the gospel,
from the beginning of the fourth century to the death
of Constantius, he says, " This should be the favourite

---

* See Mosheim and Milner, Cent. 16.

† See Bogue and Bennet's history of the Dissenters. Period 2,
Chapter iv. Section 1st.

object of a Christian historian, and glad should I be to answer the most sanguine wishes of the evangelical reader. But the period before us, is far more fruitful in ecclesiastical contentions, than remarkable for the extension of Christianity itself; and even the account which we have of the triumphs of the Redeemer's death and resurrection, in the barbarous countries, is too mean and defective, to satisfy the laudable curiosity of those who love the progress of vital religion."* The contentions of Christians, then, in this and the succeeding centuries, tended to shroud the glory of the office for whose permanence we are now contending. We might refer to other moral causes, as conducing to this end; we shall, however, in winding up this section, advert only to another, which though last, is the not least, in the dark catalogue; that is the ambition — the successful ambition — the elevation and power of the bishops. Originally, the terms bishop and presbyter were applied to the same individuals, holding office in any church. But in process of time, the term bishop was applied to one individual, who had the highest authority, in any particular community. The presbyters, or elders, were, indeed, still, in every church, but they were the inferiors of the bishops. So, also, were the deacons. These latter, are generally supposed to have been appointed to the care of the temporal affairs of the church; but the bishop so contrived, as to be not only the supreme ruler of the community, but its treasurer. Thus we see the bishop had risen to dignity, at the expence of his fellow officers. Now if such was the case with these officers, would it be surprising that he should domineer over another office, equal, if not superior, to his own, in importance, namely, the *evangelist's* ? This might arise, in the first instance, from the evangelists themselves becoming pastors over the churches they

---

* History of the Church, &c. Cent. 4, Chap. vi.

L

had collected. Christianity would be entirely new to the people composing these churches, and, consequently, the whole management of their concerns would, in a great degree, if not entirely, devolve on the missionaries who first taught them.——This we see is the case, with many missionaries, in modern times. —— If elders, and deacons also, were appointed in these churches, the influence, knowledge, and capacity, of the missionary, would lead the above officers, with the exception of the drudgery of their offices, to hold them under him as the bishop, only nominally. This might, probably, be the case, in a great many instances, and as a result of it, the missionary would unite in himself the two offices of evangelist and bishop, and, consequently, he would contend that the power of ordination belonged exclusively to him. The presbyter and evangelist of the apostolic age, ordained each other reciprocally, but when both offices were united in the person of one individual, it is only natural to suppose, that that individual would regard himself, in point of ordination, as superior to all others. Such, it was reported, had been the case with both Timothy and Titus. The one —— Timothy —— was said by Eusebius, from tradition, not scriptural authority, to be the first bishop of Ephesus ; and the other —— Titus —— the first bishop of Crete. It is, probably, owing to this, that in the Catholic, Lutheran, Anglican, and Moravian churches, we have, in their diocesan bishop, in some respects, the nearest resemblance to the ancient evangelist that is to be found, among church officers, in modern times, with the exception of those of the Methodists. This is, in all likelihood, the reason why Eusebius, in referring to the evangelists of the second century, gives us, as among them, Quadratus, bishop of Athens ; Ignatius, bishop of Antioch ; and Clemens, bishop of Rome. We know, for certain, that this was the case with Pothinus and Irenæus. They came, as missionaries, from Asia to Lyons and Vienne, and afterwards were bishops in these places. The diocesan bishop appears thus gradually to have crept into the church, and then seems to have endeavoured to foist his origin on the missions of Timothy and Titus, as evangelists to Ephesus and Crete ; forgetting that these distinguished men were sent to these places, not to be ordained bishops, but to ordain other men bishops over the churches there. Henceforward, then, we find the evangelists displaced— the scale being turned, and the right of ordination entirely usurped, by their pretended successors, under the title of bishops. It is rather a surprising circumstance that they did not choose to retain the original title. There was, surely, as much honour in the one, as in the other. Timothy was called on to do the work of an evangelist, and not that of a bishop. The office of evangelist is, also, placed before that of pastors, by Paul, in his enumeration of offices, in the fourth of Ephesians. The evangelists were also the immediate attendants on the apostles, and the duties of the former, much more resembled those of the latter, than did those of the pastors. Why, then, did they not retain the name ? The circumstance seems unaccountable, except on the score of local attachments and interests. There would be a mutual attachment between them and the people, whom they had been the means of lately converting, and inspiring with a heavenly hope. They might, also, be desirous, after years of itinerating labours, to enjoy comparative repose, in performing the duties connected with a circumscribed locality. Their desires for this would also be greatly heightened, if they had families. The title of bishop, too, had gradually been acquiring renown. The lists of the bishops in the different churches, and, especially, in the leading ones of Jerusalem, Antioch, Rome, Alexandria, Corinth, &c., had been either carefully preserved, or were pretended to be so ; whereas, on the other hand, the names of those who were merely missionaries, or evangelists, were but little noted. For such reasons, then, and it may be others, with which, at present, we are unacquainted, and perhaps, cannot easily conjecture, did these men, probably prefer the secondary to the primary title ; and thus the office of evangelist was swamped, and the title merged in that of bishop.   In this condition has it continued, in several communities, for ages ; and when the days of reformation came, partly from incorrect views of the office itself, partly from the wrong use of some of its duties, namely, *ordination* and confirmation, and the entire neglect of others, namely, missionary labour and toil, as exhibited in the diocesan bishops ; and partly, perhaps chiefly, from its great onerous duty — missiona_ry work, neither being well understood, nor acted upon, at the time, nor the obligations of the commision of Christ upon the church in general, properly felt ; all these combined, kept both the office, and its duties, in a state of complete abeyance, for a series of ages.   The day of revival, however, at length came.   The moral causes alluded to in this section, if not entirely removed, were, at least, abated.   A strong tide of missionary zeal set in.   It is still, however, to be regretted that the missionary office appears as a pious expedient, rather than a divine appointment.   In the ensuing section, these important points will claim our attention.

SECTION SEVENTH.

The office of the modern missionary can be regarded in no other light than, either as a human invention to sup_ply the deficiencies of infinite wisdom, or else, as the legitimate station, in all that was not extraordinary, of the original evangelists.

It has been already remarked, that missionary obligations seemed to be but little felt, by the reformers.   This, in all likelihood, arose from a combination of causes.   The more prominent of these, perhaps, were the following. In the first place : the circumstances in which they were placed. These, doubtless, prevented them from either thinking much of the heathen, or doing much for them. Their lives and time were wholly taken up, either in the grand struggle with the papacy in one form or other, or else they were devoted to the superintendence and scriptural instruction of the faithful, who adhered to them, after leaving the Romish community. In the second place: their previous habits were not in accordance with missionary views and feelings. It is true, that missionaries of a certain cast, had ever, more or less, been called into use, under the Church of Rome. All the west of Europe had been, at different times, converted to popery, by missionaries of one kind or another. By their exertions as home missionaries, the Dominican and Franciscan friars, had saved Rome from reformation, for two centuries before it came. The Jesuits also, as foreign missionaries, both in the eastern and western hemispheres, had exerted themselves, to make converts to the Roman see. But still, previous to the reformation, Europe, on the point of religion, was comparatively quiet; and though, in the providence of God, materials were preparing, in a variety of ways, for the great explosion, the *event* itself, a few years before it happened, was not at all anticipated; and Luther, when he began it, was little aware where it was to end. In consequence of this, matters went on in the church in the old way. Young men prepared for it, or were specially trained to it, and in process of time, were inducted into its livings. All that was then thought of was, a usual routine of service, and the chief idea that had a hold of the mind was, how to climb to a loftier eminence, than that which they at present held. To be a church dignitary, of one description or another, was the *ne plus ultra* of their ambition. The nature of the kingdom of Christ, and the spread of that kingdom, were ideas of which they were almost totally ignorant. In this way were the reformers educated. As ecclesiastics,

L 3

they knew scarcely anything but parish duty, or the recluse religious services of the monastery.

But, in the third place, not only their habits but their views, prevented them from taking such an active part in missions, as has been taken since. They did not conceive that they were obligated to preach to the heathen. There was no office in the church appointed for so doing, and therefore the heathen must wait to be instructed in the knowledge of salvation, till God in his providence raised up men for the purpose; which he sometimes did, said they, as apostles, or, at least, as evangelists. Such were the views of Calvin, who had as large an influence in guiding the conceptions of the reformers, as any single individual whatever. "They that have the government of the church," says he, "according to the institute of Christ, are named by Paul. First, apostles, then, prophets, thirdly, evangelists, fourthly, pastors, and last of all, teachers. Of these, the two last alone have ordinary office in the church: the other three the Lord set up, at the beginning of his kingdom, and *sometimes even yet, as the necessity of the times may require.*" Again, with regard to evangelists, he says, "By evangelists I understand those, who, though in *dignity*, they were *less* than the apostles, yet, in office, they were next unto them, yea, and even occupied their room. Such were Luke, Timothy, Titus, &c.; and perhaps, also, the seventy disciples, whom Christ appointed in the second place after the apostles. According to this exposition, which seemeth to me agreeable both to the words and meaning of Paul—these three offices were not ordained in the church to the end, that they should be perpetual, but only to serve for that time wherein churches were to be erected, where there were none before, or at least, to be removed from Moses to Christ." "Although," he adds, "I deny not, but that afterward also the Lord hath sometimes raised up apostles or, at least, in their places, evangelists, as it hath been done in our time; for it is needful to have such to bring back *the church* from the falling away to antichrist : yet the office itself, I do nevertheless call extraordinary, because it hath no place in the churches already well set in order."[*]

The name of Calvin, doubtless, stands deservedly high as a scripture expositor, but we confess, with all due deference to so high an authority, that the above view of the office of an evangelist, appears to us a very confused and contradictory one. He says, indeed, justly, that the object of their appointment was the erection of churches, or, at least, in order to these churches being removed from Moses to Christ. He might have added, and from Baal to God. They were also to occupy the room of the apostles, that is, we suppose, occupy their place after they were dead, as well as when they were absent, whilst living. But still the office was not to be perpetual, and yet God had raised up some in his time, to call the Christian world back from antichrist. Here he surely must refer to such as Luther and himself, although modesty prevented him from mentioning it. But may it not be justly asked, Were there not other churches to be erected after Timothy and Titus were laid in their graves, as well as those churches that *they* had erected? To say nothing of many to be brought from Baal to God, there were many still to be brought from Moses to Christ. And if God raised up evangelists, at the time of the reformation, to bring back the church from the falling away to antichrist, are there not many still connected with the professing church of Christ, that need to be brought back from that same antichrist? And if such are not needed in churches already well set in order — there are still many persons, in different parts of the world, that need, by the preaching of the gospel, to be prepared in order to be members of churches; and it is still necessary that churches, composed of such in-

---

[*] Institutes, Book IV. Chap. iii. Sec. 4.

dividuals, should, by evangelists, be well set in order.

Such, then, were Calvin's opinions on this subject, when he published the last edition of his institutes, in 1558; and a somewhat similar opinion was entertained and expressed by Dr. Owen, in a work which he finished a short time before his death, in 1683. In proposing the question—Whether a man may be ordained a pastor or minister, without a relation unto any particular church, so as to be invested with "office power," he replies, 1. "It is granted that a man endowed with spiritual gifts "—by which we suppose he means natural and cultivated talents for the preaching of the gospel —" may be set apart by fasting and prayer to that work, when he may be orderly *called* to it in the providence of God: for such an one hath a *call materially* in the gifts which he hath received, and *setting him apart is a moral duty*; and, as a *public testimony*, is necessary, first on his own account, that he may be received by the churches which he may visit, and second, that the churches themselves may not be imposed on. 2. Such persons, so set apart, may be esteemed ministers in the general notion of the word, and may be useful in the calling and planting of churches, wherein they may be installed in the pastoral office. This was, originally, the *work of evangelists : which office being ceased in the church, may be supplied by persons of this sort. 3. No church whatever hath power to ordain men ministers for the conversion of infidels. Since the cessation of extraordinary officers and offices, the care of the work is devolved merely on the providence of God, being left without the verge of church institutions.* God alone can send and warrant men for the undertaking of that work. Nor can any man know, or be satisfied, in a call unto that work, without some previous guidance, by divine providence leading him thereto. It is, indeed, the *duty of all ordinary ministers of the church to diffuse the knowledge of Christ and the gospel unto the heathen and infidels among whom, or near to whom, their habitation* is cast, and they have *all manner of divine warranty for their doing so ; as many worthy persons have done effectually in New England. And it is the duty of every true Christian, who may be cast among them, in the providence of God, to instruct them, according to his ability, in the knowledge of the truth.* But it is not in the power of any church, or any sort of ordinary officers, to ordain a person to the office of the ministry for the conversion of the heathen antecedently unto any designation by divine providence thereunto. 4. *No man can be properly or completely ordained to the ministry but he that is ordained to a determinate office, such as a bishop, an elder, or pastor :* for 1. This would be contrary to the constant practice of the apostles, who ordained no ordinary officers but in particular churches, which were their proper charge. 2. It was absolutely forbidden in the ancient church, as in the case of Eustathius, bishop of Pamphylia. 3. Such an ordination wants an essential constitutive cause, in the absence of the election of the people. 4. A bishop, elder, or pastor, being terms of relation, so, to make one who has no such relation, is a direct contradiction. 5. It is inconsistent with the nature and end of the pastoral office." *

We entertain the highest opinion both of the character and abilities of Dr. Owen, but still we think, in the passage cited, he does not appear to the greatest advantage. To say the least of it, it appears like that of his great master Calvin, confused, if not contradictory. In the first place: the Doctor grants us *all we are pleading for. A person, he says, may do the work of an evangelist, call and plant churches, even in these modern days.* This is conceding, at once, that the work is ordinary work, adapted to all times, and confined to none. And not only so, but a man may have a special *call* in *provi-*

---

* The true nature of a gospel church. Chap V. On the duty of pastors of churches.

dence to this *work,* and *this call may be easily ascertained
by the gifts he possesses, or, in other words, his capacity
for the work:* and further still, he may be *ordained*
under these circumstances, and this *ordination* is a *moral
duty,* both on the *man's own account,* and on *account of
the churches of Christ in general, that he may be accepted
of them, and they not imposed on by him.* This is, to
the full, what we are contending for ; but mark how
the good Doctor immediately upsets the whole. Such
an office, he says, is beyond the verge of church
institutions, since the cessation of extraordinary officers
and offices, of which the evangelist's office was one.
The *conversion of infidels,* and, of course, *missionary
work,* is work wholly belonging to the *providence of
God, and churches have nothing to do in the matter,*
except under an *especial call ;* and, even then, a man,
though ordained, cannot be regarded as completely so,
as he is not a *bishop,* or *pastor,* or elder, having a particular charge, and sustaining a particular relation to a
people, by whom he has been regularly called to pastoral duty among them. All this, he says, is opposed
both to *scripture,* and the *usage* of the *ancient church,*
who never regarded an individual as a bishop unless
he held a particular charge. It is evident from all this,
that the Doctor, though an *original,* and *independent*
thinker, and one who gave evidence above many, of his
deference to divine authority, was still under the influence of prejudice, with regard to ministerial ordination,
extraordinary endowments, and the offices of the primitive labourers. In all he says, he never once adverts to
the commission of Christ, as being of lasting obligation,
nor yet to the wisdom of God, as furnishing means to
the attainment of this end. No one has written better
than he on the wisdom of God, in fixing on means to
accomplish ends ; as is evident from the interesting
chapter in his work on the person of Christ, which he
intitles, "A humble enquiry into the infinite wisdom of
God, in the constitution of the person of Christ." He

also makes no discrimination between extraordinary, and ordinary times, and work; neither does he advert to the important enquiry, how far *ordinary*, may supply the lack of *extraordinary* means? This is the case, both in the work referred to, and in his "Discourses on the Holy Spirit, and his work," where extraordinary gifts and offices are more particularly alluded to. The Doctor, also, omits to notice the difference between the ordination of stationary and ambulatory teachers. The scriptures certainly speak of both. They speak of the ordination of Timothy, as well as of the ordination of both bishops and deacons. They allude also to the extraordinary call of the bishops, by the Holy Ghost; to their work; to their extraordinary endowments; and to their working under the eye and guidance of the apostles; as well as to the endowments, &c. of the evangelist. But the Doctor overlooks all these important points in the discussion, and seems to have too much taken for granted, what appear to us, the too superficial views which, by certain writers of note, had been entertained, previously, on the subject.

The prejudices of the Doctor on this subject, are, however, not so much to be wondered at, when we reflect that not only the writers of his own age, but almost all previous and subsequent writers, take the same view of the subject. We cannot, however, but respect the motives by which he was influenced, in taking the views he did. These motives were, his respect for the scriptures and the authority of God. Christian churches, he conceived, were the only appointed means for the conversion of the world, and the only officers he found connected with churches, were pastors, and teachers, and deacons. These were the only institutions found within the verge of the churches; and, consequently, whatever other appointment was now made, was, as he conceived, a human device—an intrusion on fixed order—and, consequently, an insult to the King of Zion. Now who is there that can do otherwise than respect all this? and where is the person that can prove he is wrong with respect to his conclusions, provided his premises are correct? If, indeed, the evangelist's office is not a permanent institution, but only a temporary one, then, indeed, there are no officers to go to preach to infidels, as the only officers now in existence are, by their charge, and their duties, confined to certain localities. With all this, however, it is almost amusing to observe the workings of the Doctor's feelings. He cannot but think it the duty of any person living not far from where the heathen are, to tell them of the way of salvation. He also highly applauds those who, lately, in New England, had acted on this principle. In this, we see the truth of the remark, "that the hearts of some men will sometimes carry them further than their heads will allow." The Doctor's heart would have led him either to be a missionary, or to send out missionaries, but his head — his views of the evangelist's office, and the constitution of a Christian church — would not allow him. Such is the one-sided view the Doctor has taken of the subject. It is anticipating time by a hundred years, yet, we cannot help noticing here, the view taken by another distinguished individual, namely, Dr. Carey, on the other side. In his ever memorable "Enquiry into the obligations of Christians to use means for the conversion of the heathen," Dr. Carey endeavours to prove the permanency of the commission of Christ. His arguments are the following. 1. "If we are not to carry the gospel to the heathen, we ought equally to renounce baptism, as the one was given to be performed by inspired and endowed men, as well as the other. 2. All ordinary ministers, who have endeavoured to carry the gospel to the heathen, have acted without a warrant ; yea, and though God has promised the most glorious things to the heathen world, by sending the gospel to them, yet, whoever goes with that message, unless he have a new and special commision from heaven, must go without any authority for so doing. 3. The extent of the command must be gathered from the extent of the promise "Lo I am with you alway, even to the end of the world." Dr. Carey then proceeds to shew that there are cases in which a divine command may cease to be binding. 1. The repeal of the law, as in the case of the Jewish dispensation. 2. The failure of its subjects: as in the case of the septennial release, when there was no poor they could not have their debts forgiven. Deut. xv. 4. 3. A counter-revelation: as in the case of Paul not being suffered by the Spirit to go to Bithynia. Acts xvi. 7. 4. Natural impossibility: as in the case of Paul going to Otaheite, which was not then discovered. None of these circumstances, he affirms, can be pleaded by Christians, as an excuse for disobeying our Lord's commission."* Now all this seems very forcible. The perpetuity of the commission is proved beyond a doubt, and Dr. Owen would accede to this, and say the thing will be done. God in his good time will raise up and qualify men for the work ; but still it is not obligatory on his church, whom he has furnished with no officers for the purpose. As to baptism, it may be performed by ordinary officers, as others besides the apostles baptized. Here then is a dilemma. The one good man proves there is work that ought to be done by the church ; the other affirms there is not any one appointed to do it. Dr. Carey does not meet Dr. Owen's difficulty. It only can be met, we apprehend, by denying Dr. Owen's premises, in the way of shewing, that there are officers appointed to do this work, namely, the evangelists ; and that all he affirms in opposition to their permanence, may be equally affirmed, in opposition to the permanence of those whom he really allows to be permanent, namely, the pastors of the churches. This idea may have been suggested to the Doctor by others in his own day ; but if so, he still

---

* See Carey's Enquiry, &c. pages 8, 9, 10.

M

clung to Calvin's opinion, that churches well set in order, need not evangelists, as these lie beyond the range of its officers.

Is it at all surprising, then, that there should have been so little missionary exertion at the time of the Reformation, and also for such a length of time after it? The circumstances, then, of the Protestants, their previous habits, and their confused views and prejudices, respecting missionary labour, and missionary labourers, account sufficiently for it. What was actually attempted and done, even under these circumstances, is not, however, to be forgotten. In the year 1556, there were sent, not fewer than fourteen missionaries from Geneva, to plant the Christian faith, in the newly discovered regions of America. These are supposed to have formed part of a French colony of Protestant refugees in Brazil, and which untoward circumstances unhappily speedily terminated. All the protestants were speedily murdered by the catholics in the neighbourhood. These missionaries must have been sent out from Geneva, under the eye of Calvin. He, probably, from his views, already stated, looked upon them as evangelists, specially raised up by providence, for the work in which they embarked. The next missionary attempt that we read of was in Lapland, under the auspices of the celebrated Gustavas Vasa, King of Sweden. This was in 1559. Then, in the beginning of the seventeenth century, the missions of the Dutch to the East India colonies. After this, the attempts in America of the pilgrim fathers, — who had fled from persecution in Britain,— to instruct the Indians in their vicinity, in the principles of Christianity. This took place about 1642. From that period to the end of the seventeenth century, the work was in progress, and many Indians were brought under the influence of Christianity, by Mayhew, Eliot, Brainerd, and others. In the beginning of the eighteenth century, the Danes sent two missionaries to the coast of Coromandel, in the East Indies ; and about the same time, a Mr. Hans Egede, a Dane, went out as a missionary to Greenland. After having been there for about fifteen years, all his labours appeared abortive, and he returned to Denmark, with an almost broken heart. This appeared very mysterious, and very unlike the fulfilment of the promise, "Lo I am with you alway, even to the end of the world." *Mysterious, however, as it appeared, from the very failure of that mission, by a wonderful chain of circumstances, mysteriously linked together, have preceded the numerous missions of the times in which we live.* Count Zinzendorff, the bishop of the united brethren, or Moravians, was at Copenhagen, when Mr. Egede returned from his unsuccessful mission, and heard of it. His heart was touched with sympathy, especially when he saw two of the native Greenlanders that had been baptized by Mr. Egede. He returned to Hernhuth, the Moravian settlement, and imbued the minds of the brethren with the idea of a mission to Greenland ; and in 1733, Christian David, and two others, went out as missionaries, to its cold inhospitable shores. About the same time, others went to the West India islands, to teach the negroes the way of salvation, and to make them, in the midst of their bondage, "free, with the liberty with which Christ makes his people free." It was in company with a number of these missionaries, in the year 1735, that Mr. John Wesley first became acquainted with the way of salvation, through Christ, as "the Lord our righteousness." These men shewed him not only how to die with tranquility, but also how best to live efficiently, as a missionary labourer in the service of God. He afterward became useful to thousands, by innoculating them with the same spirit. Among these may be numbered the late Dr. Thomas Coke. This good man became connected with Mr. Wesley's people in 1778, and in 1786 sailed from England for Nova

Scotia. Providentially, however, the vessel in which he sailed, was driven to the West Indies. They landed on the island of Antigua; and the Doctor and his three companions resolved to commence a mission here, and the neighbouring islands. God had been preparing the way already for their reception. Nathaniel Gilbert, Esq., Speaker of the House of Assembly. in the island of Antigua, to whom Mr. Wesley had been made useful, when in England, had, on his return, taught the negroes in his own house. He died, and left a Mr. Baxter at the head of the society. When Dr. Coke came among them, he found that "the fields were white already to harvest, and in this, and the adjacent islands, has many a plenteous harvest since been gathered into the garner of God.

Dr. Coke may, in a certain degree, be said to have been the father of British missions. He not only paved the way for the present extended exertions of the Methodist missionary society, but he was useful in preparing the way for others. It was in hearing a sermon preached by him, that the late Samuel Pearce of Birmingham, one of the first committee of the Baptist mission, had his mind first imbued, as he himself terms it, with a *"passion for missions;"* and the publication of the *deeply interesting memoir* of this *truly pious man,* tended, materially, to increase the popularity of the mission cause in this country. The Baptist mission had its rise in 1792. Its germ was a prayer meeting, established in 1784, in the midland counties. The late Dr. Carey, from whose Enquiry, printed about this time, we have before given an extract, was its mainspring; and he met with a powerful supporter in Mr. Fuller, afterwards the secretary of the society. The London missionary society followed, in 1795. The Scottish mission followed soon after; and the beginning of the nineteenth century saw the rise of the church missionary society, in England. Other societies of a like description speedily followed, both on the continent of Europe and in America.*

The missionaries employed by all these different societies, by this time, are very numerous, and occupy different fields of labour, in various parts of the world. Their work, in all its main features, is the very work in which the primitive missionaries engaged. They are not called, like the apostles, to reveal the will of God to their fellow-creatures, but they translate the scriptures into the languages of the countries they visit. They preach the same immortal truth — " the truth as it is in Jesus" — to their ignorant fellow-creatures. They lead the enquirers among them to the Saviour of the guilty. They baptize the penitent believers. They incorporate all such into a spiritual body; calling upon them to watch over each other in love. They lead them to the choice of spiritual guides, who may superintend their affairs, and be the means, under God, of building them up on their most holy faith. They endeavour to train, from among the young converts, those who are likely to be useful, as missionaries, to their own countrymen, and to carry on the work of God, in their native land, when the missionary fathers have retired to their everlasting rest. Such, for substance, is the character of the mass of missionaries now in the field; to select any for particular illustration would be invidious. As far as the *work* of all of them is concerned, they are, *essentially, evangelists.* Now the question is, *In what light are they to be regarded? Are they to be looked on as the successors of the evangelists?— their legitimate successors in all things, not extraordinary, and peculiar to the age in which they lived; or are they to be regarded as a class of men, superinduced on divine institu-*

---

* See Brown's History of the Propagation of Christianity; and Stowell's Missionary Church. Pearce's Memoirs, by Fuller; and the Periodical accounts of the different missionary societies.

tions, by the sagacity of man, to supply the deficiencies of the wisdom of God? In the one light, or the other, they must, doubtless, be viewed. They are either appointed by God, or by man. God, however, has not left appointments in his kingdom to the discretion of men. Had He merely *made known* to us the gospel, and said it *was adapted for all, and free to all,* we *then,* might have *used our prudence, in reference to the best way of spreading the knowledge of it ;* but this is not the case : as our *Sovereign,* in all cases, has furnished us, not only *with an end to be gained, but means whereby to attain it ;* as he has furnished an amplitude of means, with relation both to the converted and unconverted, in his word, and which were employed, with efficiency, at the commencement of the Christian era ; it is, surely, befitting man, as a weak and erring creature, to try his maker's methods, before he has recourse to his own. Should he prove, by experience, his maker to be unwise, he may then try his own skill ; but, certainly, modesty should lead him to make the trial first. Let us apply this to the subject in hand. If God has exhibited a class of men, in his word, fitted for the enlightenment and conversion of the world, as well as a class adapted to instruct and watch over the faithful ; surely the one class were intended to be employed, as well as the other. There may, indeed, have been circumstances, peculiar in their character, at the time when both classes were summoned into being and use ; and these peculiar circumstances, so far modified them at the time, as to prevent a complete identification, at any future period ; still, as the work peculiar to both classes, is work adapted for every part, and every age, of the world, it is, surely, becoming the creatures of God to honour both his authority and his wisdom, by cheerfully adopting them, and constantly using them. But if, on the other hand, we suppose that God has presented an object before us — say that that object is the conversion of the world in every age — and, at the same time, has furnished us with no means to attain this object, we certainly pay no compliment to his intelligence. If we suppose that He has left the accomplishment of that work, which, of all others, is intended to redound most to his glory, *to the wisdom and prudence of men*, we, most assuredly, tarnish his glory, by divesting him of an attribute which it is his highest honour to wear. But we do this, we humbly conceive, when we affirm that the office of a missionary is *not one of divine appointment* — that it is *beyond the verge of the institutions of his kingdom ; and that it has no precise type, in the New Testament, for its guidance*. We may, indeed, with an air of piety, throw its existence and use, in these modern days, on the *providence of God*, thus relieving his church from doing that, which he has positively commanded to be done, in every age ; but such piety, as it is devoid of conferring benefit on man, so it is equally remote from bestowing honour upon God. Our conclusion, then, seems inevitable, namely, that the modern missionary, can be regarded in no other light, than either, as a human invention, to supply the deficiences of infinite wisdom ; or else, as the legitimate successor, in all that is not extraordinary, of the original evangelist.

We shall conclude the present section by a quotation from the able work of Mr. Macleod, formerly alluded to. After citing what Dr. Owen says respecting no church having power to ordain men ministers, for the conversion of infidels, since the cessation of extraordinary officers and offices, the care of these being devolved on the providence of God, and so left, without the verge of church institutions,—Mr. M. makes the following remarks. "On the supposition that the evangelist's office was extraordinary, the above reasoning, which indicates a mind accustomed to pay the profoundest deference to the word and the authority of God, is plainly unanswerable. It is, indeed, little accordant to the happy missionary spirit of the present period. And were the Doctor now alive, would he not display the benevolence of his great and ardent mind in missionary efforts, and recognize them as essentially arising from the permanent institutions of the church? But if the work of missionaries has the sanction of scripture, (and who can deny this?) there must be an appropriate scriptural designation found for them, as an order of teachers whose peculiar work is still within the verge of church institutions. As to the term missionary, it is admitted to be a good enough translation of the Greek term for apostle. The application of it to those who now preach among the heathen, is unsanctioned by the usage of scripture. Neither is preacher, or teacher, a name which, according to scripture, can be appropriated to missionaries, because each of these terms is applied to others, who also preached and taught the doctrine of Christ. The only distinct class of teachers to whom missionaries bear any resemblance, is evangelists. We may refuse them the name, but God has assigned them a work, which was of old " the work of an evangelist." And it is pleasing to observe, that the conductors of missionary and evangelical institutions, have begun to apply their appropriate and distinctive designation to their brethren, whose work it is to evangelize the world."

" It were altogether absurd, after what " God hath wrought" in our own day, to suppose that, of the living instruments employed to propagate the gospel at first, none were left to illuminate the remaining darkness of the world. Had the early Christians been of this mind, would the gospel have spread so extensively after the days of the apostles? Men still ran "to and fro," to increase the knowledge of the Lord, and they turned many to righteousness. Is it not exceedingly incongruous to believe in the approaching glory of the millenial period, and to disbelieve that any specific means are appointed of God, to illuminate the nations? Has God, indeed, contrary to all the rest of his procedure, left so great a matter to our discretion and ingenuity; or is there nothing definite in scripture with respect to the instruments by which this great work has been so auspiciously commenced, and by which it will, doubtless, be gloriously consummated? Are evangelists less necessary to extend and consolidate the kingdom of Christ, than pastors are to rule and feed the churches over which they are appointed overseers? In the civil, military, and commercial affairs of mankind, are not similar distinctions of office required, relative to domestic and foreign concerns? Of the same army, some "go forth to battle, and some abide by the stuff." And it was a law of David, that these should share alike in the enterprize." *

These ideas will be found somewhat more expanded in the succeeding section, where the work remaining yet to be done, will be shown to demonstrate the continuance of the office in question, as a permanent institution of the kingdom of Christ.

SECTION EIGHTH.

The work that still remains to be accomplished, in the Christian conquest of the world, is one that requires the utmost weight to attach, not only to the character, but to the office, of those principally engaged in achieving it.

The conquest of the world to the spiritual sceptre of of the Redeemer, is an event which prophecy places within the expectation of the church. The language of the prophesies of the Old Testament on the subject, is rich and glowing. An inexpressible delight steals through the mind in reading them, and we can scarcely resist the idea of seeing the whole of the magnificent picture pass before us. Eden in all its luxuriousness, and all its peacefulness, without exhibiting a single

---

* Macleod's View of Inspiration, &c., Ch 19, P. 493 and 495.

blight, or echoing a single growl, is almost forgotten, in the sacred thrill of joy with which the mind is fraught, when, in the latter days, it sees broken swords and shattered spears all surrounding the forge, ready to be beat into plough-shares and pruning hooks; and this too combined with little children frolicking with the wild beasts of the desert, and putting their hands on the cockatrice's den.   All this, however, we are told, shall be exhibited, and exhibited too, in the midst of scenery, the most enchanting — a sky without a cloud, the ocean without a warlike galley — and the earth in no spot discovering in its produce, the slightest trace of its maker's frown.   Surely philanthropy, high as its desires are, in the midst of such a scene as this, must feel its most unbounded wishes gratified.

Now, all this is said to result from the spread of the gospel.   "The knowledge of the Lord shall cover the earth, as the waters cover the sea."   "Men also shall be blessed in the Saviour; and all nations shall call him blessed."   "From the rising of the sun to the going down of the same, incense and a pure offering shall be presented to the name of the Lord."   The general circulation of the scriptures, and the preaching of the gospel of the grace of God, shall tend not only to reconcile *God and man*, but they will also tend to reconcile *men to each other*.   The grand characteristic of this period, as celebrated even by angels, was, and still is, "Glory to God in the highest, on earth peace, and good will to men."

When we consult the more unpoetical books of the New Testament, we find the same circumstances all presented to the faith and hope of Christians.   The apostle, for instance, in the eleventh chapter of his epistle to the Romans, speaking of the ingathering of the Jews, in connexion with the fulness of the Gentiles, plainly intimates the coming of a time when the majority of the world, to say the least of it, shall be brought under the influence of pure and undefiled religion; and thus, earth shall become a little heaven, "Righteousness and peace and joy in the Holy Ghost," being the general order of the day.

Such are the hopes and joyful expections of the Christian church : and these hopes, we rejoice to think, have, even already, in a measure, been realized. The various efforts of the different missionary societies, have already extended the Christian name and religion, into regions where they were before scarcely ever heard of. It is only little more than three hundred years since the one half of the earth was discovered. But when the *crown of the world*, according to ancient prophecy and promise, was about to be put on the Redeemer's head, the *whole*, hitherto concealed for ages, and generations, *is made known to man*. A Genoese sailor, being sent by providence, like Cyrus to open the two leaved gates, discovered it. The dim dawn of the Millenial day began at the reformation, and the long "day of the Lord," which is "as a thousand years," by the gradual breaking away of the shadows of the preceding gloomy night, is fast coming onward. The sun of righteousness, ere long, will be seen tinging with his rosy hues the eastern hills, and marching on in the greatness of his strength, rejoicing as a strong man to run his race, will shine more and more unto the perfect day. It is a remarkable circumstance, that, even now, the greater portion of the globe is under the government of states professedly Christian. And what is more remarkable still, such is the case, even with the greatest portion of human beings. Surely, then, the signs of the times indicate, that the coming of the Lord is at no great distance. Already Mahomedanism totters to its base, and the darkness of heathenism is dispelling. In the east, the Bible has been partially translated into forty languages and dialects. A number of Christian churches also are scattered over Hindostan and Burmah ; China itself, also, can number both its missionaries and its believers. The isles of the pacific are not merely waiting, but have actually received, the Saviour's law. The discovery of the interior of Africa, will not only lead to the extension of commerce, but commerce, in in its turn, will pave the way for the gospel. The cross is already erected in the south of that continent, at the cape, and Ethiopia, in the east, is, in reality, stretching out her hands to God. The whole earth, in short, is in motion. Education is spreading — the Bible is circulating — and prejudices are giving way on every hand. "The light of the moon is becoming as the light of the sun, and the light of the sun as the light of seven days: and the Lord of hosts is about to reign in mount Zion, and in Jerusalem, and before his ancients gloriously."

But though much has been done, still more remains to be accomplished. Though many missionaries have been sent forth, more still are needed. If we reckon them all up who are now employed, we shall not find a thousand missionaries, from all parties, in heathen lands. To say nothing of the other continents, or of the interesting isles of the pacific, the teeming millions of Asia, are calling aloud for our help. The field is, indeed, a mighty one — not less than the world. What an extensive harvest, and how few to reap it! What our Lord said when he sent out the seventy is still true, "The harvest is truly plenteous, but the labourers are few; pray ye therefore the Lord of the harvest that He would thrust forth more labourers into his harvest." More labourers, most assuredly, are wanted. It will be long before the world be in the state that even Britain is, in a Christian point of view. And, even then, how far will it be from what we expect! The Christian church will need to pray more, and to contribute more, than it ever has done, by a thousand fold, before a sufficient number of missionaries be placed, and kept, in the field. Many missionaries, whose hearts God has touched, and inclined, and fitted for the work, will have to present themselves. In order to perform their work efficiently, too, such missionaries would, each and all need to sustain a *Christian character* of the most exalted kind. They would need to be men of active habits, of great prudence, of undaunted courage, or, at least, of moral heroism.—Men to whom " God has not given the spirit of fear, but of power, and of love, and of a sound mind." Such were the primitive mission-aries, and such men only shall be able to realize the promises of God in the scriptures, and the hopes of the Christian church. These primitive missionaries, within the space of thirty years, " turned the world upside down." Wherever they went, they made, if the phrase may be allowed, a *moral earthquake*. They headed " a sect" that was every where spoken about, and " every where spoken against," as being ever restless in its obtrusions into the dark domains of sin and error. What a number, through their instrumentality, were actually brought out of darkness into marvellous light, and from the service of dumb idols, to the service of the living and the true God! Like the Corinthians, thousands, through their means, before the destruction of Jerusa-lem, " were washed, and sanctified, and justified, in the name of the Lord Jesus, and by the spirit of our God." And we have no hesitation in saying, that if a suitable number of such men were embarked in the same work, even without their extraordinary endowments, before other thirty years passed over the world, such moral wonders would be effected as would far exceed the most sanguine expectations of those who might live to witness them. All missionary societies, then, ought to be especially careful in selecting men of the right character. Much of their usefulness depends on this. All may not have the high qualities of a Brainerd, a Swartz, or a Carey; but still there must be a near approximation to these, or they had better remain at home.

Important, however, as it is, to have men of the right character to be missionaries, it is equally, if not more important, to have their office placed on a proper foundation. That office must not be left, in regard to its use, to either the whim of individuals, or the caprice of either doing its work, or not, on the part of religious societies. No: it is too important, too extensive, and too sacred for this. It will require the united energies of the whole Christian church, working heart and hand, to perform it. At the present pace of missionary success, many—many years will have to roll away, and many a generation will have to be laid beneath the green sward, before the conversion of the world be accomplished. It is of the utmost consequence, then, in order to the word of the Lord " running, having free course, and being glorified," that, as much as possible, every let, every hinderance, be removed out of the way. Many of these have been removed, but some still remain. It is now generally allowed, that missionary work is permanent, and obligatory on the church of God. Not only is this allowed, but it is acted upon. Almost all denominations of Christians are now in the field; and many persons, in various parts of the world, through their means, have been enlightened. We hope this will continue, and even increase; but still there may be a declension. The church declined in piety, and relaxed its zeal in doing good, after the first century, and who can tell what may be its state at the end of the present century? It may decline, and that declension may be accelerated by the idea, that the missionary is not a scriptural officer. Besides; there is reason to fear that some, at least, are still prevented from joining heart and hand in the work of missions, from the operation of the principle of good Dr. Owen —— that the mission cause ought to be left to providence; and that those only should engage in the work, who have a clear and undeniable call in providence to engage in it; as no office is yet found scripturally within the verge of church institutions, statedly to accomplish it. It is, therefore, of no small consequence to set at rest, if possible, the scriptural nature of the missionary's office, and to shew that it is within the range of church institutions, for the conversion of the world, and not merely left to the operations of providence.

Nothing is more adapted to lead to error in thinking, extravagance in feeling, or eccentricity in action, than to be guided by mental impressions, and to follow what may be deemed, under these impressions — *providential calls.* Even some great men have occasionally fallen into error here. Perhaps those two great men, Wesley and Whitfield, were not altogether exempt from this description of error. Each of them believed that he had an especial call from God, to do what he did ; and we have no wish to deny it. Indeed, now that the day of prejudice, in reference to these distinguished individuals, has gone by, it will be pretty generally acknowledged that God did raise them up to accomplish the work they achieved. They described, however, an eccentric orbit, and ought not to be regarded as models in all respects. As every planet in the celestial firmament, has its own appointed circle, to describe around its own centre, so every star in the firmament of grace has its own regular orbit appointed it, by the God of the Bible. We would make all allowance for some men under particular circumstances ; but still we must be on our guard against all wild, erratic, and wayward courses, on account of their uncontrollable tendencies. It is not, therefore, with particular individuals we have so much to do, as to guard against an improper principle. We wish to rescue the work of God — the regeneration of the world — the gathering together into one all the children of God that are scattered abroad, from the hands of enthusiasm, and to put it into the hands of a class of officers connected with the cause of God, appointed for the specific purpose of achieving it ;— a class of officers whose operation will be found no less in accordance with the scriptures, and the genius of Christianity, than, on close inspection, with the common sense of mankind.

We have seen that the views entertained by some of the leading men, at the period of the reformation, respecting the evangelist's office, was one great cause of missionary work not being undertaken by them. Church officers were provided for the converted, but not for the unconverted, these latter being left to divine providence. Now, had it been a worldly matter, and left to their own prudence, it is not likely they would have gone about it in this way. Had they been warriors, intent upon the conquest of any particular country, they never would have thought, in the first instance, of sending into that country a number of officers, to superintend certain garrisons, before any one fortress, or even any part of the country, was conquered. No: they would have sent a well appointed army of warriors to conquer the country, in the first place; and when that was achieved, they would then have put superintending officers into the subdued garrisons. And if they were still intent on the conquest of other lands, they would then have led their victorious army into another country. As worldly men, intent upon accomplishing a worldly object, this is the way they would have acted. Now, it is a very remarkable circumstance, that this was the principle upon which Mr. Wesley conducted the religious movement which took its rise more particularly under his auspices, during the last century. It would appear, from his attachment to the episcopal establishment of the country, that he never contemplated, at least in the first instance, any new plan of church polity. If, however, he did not plan it, or design it, he actually accomplished it. The machinery of Methodism is, evidently different from the machinery of episcopacy, at least, as it exists in this country. Now, how was he led to it? We apprehend in a very great degree by accidental circumstances, prudently met and directed. Being driven from the pulpits of the establishment, and viewing the state of religion in that establishment, as being at the lowest ebb, and, also, observing that it was not much better among the dissenters, owing to the deadening influence of the Arian question and other circumstances, at that period, he looked upon England as little better than a heathen country. Following the example of his great coadjutor, Whitfield, he betook himself to preaching in the open air — proclaiming repentance toward God, and faith toward our Lord Jesus Christ. He did so with good effect. Many were converted, and came and confessed, and shewed their deeds, like the Ephesians. This was the case in many parts of the kingdom. Those that were serious met together for prayer and religious conference. By this time, Mr. Wesley saw increasingly the wants of the country, and engaged a number of the new converts, who had abilities for the work, to assist him in preaching. These he distributed in different parts of the country, to describe certain circuits, for a given period. This they did, two and two. Their object was the conversion of all around them. Those who were converted, were placed under leaders, who, to use Mr. Wesley's own words, were " to OVERLOOK (episcopise) the rest." The different societies of converts thus formed, according to their ability, entertained the preachers in their houses, while travelling their circuits, and otherwise contributed to their support. Now all this arose out of circumstances.

Mr. Wesley was, in an eminent degree, possessed of the intellectual quality of sagacity. He was uncommonly shrewd, orderly, active, and untiring. He, in consequence, generally saw, on an emergency, what was wanted, and applied the remedy. In connexion, however, with his natural capabilities, we are not to forget, there can be no doubt, that Mr. Wesley was divinely assisted, in his plans and movements. He was a man of prayer — of believing, sincere, and ardent prayer; and no man of this description, has ever prayed in vain. God heard him, no doubt, and so far directed him. Connected with the good found in the best of men, there is, notwithstanding, in all some latent evil. This ac-

N 3

counts sufficiently for the failures of all men, more or less, in some things. We have already remarked, that both Mr. Wesley, and his fellow-labourer, Mr. Whitfield, were liable to misconstrue the providence of God, in relation to themselves, and to suppose that they had an extraordinary call, in some things, but which call appeared at the time, very doubtful to others, and in some instances, at length, was evidently so, to themselves. With all that was good about them both, they were, therefore, yet liable to error.— While we, therefore, allow Mr. Wesley a great deal on the score of piety, we do not think his views were correct in all things. On the contrary, we think he failed, in some important points. Yet still, in those above specified, we think he hit on ideas that were not only wonderfully wise, in a natural point of view, but also wonderfully primitive. Who does not see a striking similarity, in some things, between his mode of action, and that of the Saviour himself? When our Lord was not allowed to preach in the Jewish synagogues, he betook himself to the open air. Those impressed by what he did and said, came to him privately, and were instructed by him. Afterward, some of these were called out to preach. They had circuits given them, and so had the seventy, that were called to assist them. These were hospitably entertained by the pious, wherever they went, and otherwise supported by them ; for in their journies they never lacked any thing. The cause was carried on, in much the same manner, after our Lord ascended on high. He qualified some to be missionaries, to preach to the unconverted ; and he qualified others, to take charge of the converted. The first, were ambulatory labourers, removing from place to place, and often describing certain circuits. In these, they preached to the unconverted, and the parties who, through their means, were converted, were placed under those who were qualified to overlook and guide them. Such was the genius of Christianity. Such is its structure, considered as a whole. There are evidently in it the highest marks of wisdom. There is nothing redundant, nothing defective. Every thing is in its place. That is not first, that should be last; nor that behind, which should have been before. We may truly say respecting the religion our Redeemer has given us, in respect to its design, and the means of accomplishing it, as was said in the days of his flesh, respecting his miracles, " He hath done all things well."

The writer of these remarks is not a Methodist. There are some parts of Methodism he does not admire ; but he would neither do himself justice, nor yet the father of Methodism, as he is called, if he did not state his honest convictions, respecting both him, and, also, some parts of the outline of that system which will immortalize his name. The grand feature of the system is — it is essentially missionary. On other systems, we see missionary labour superinduced, but not found in them, as an integral part. In Methodism, it is the soul of the system. We have no hesitation, also, in saying, that it is the soul of the Christian system; and where it is wanting, in any denomination, that denomination, in that point, is essentially wrong.

Here, then, we may again return to the reformers. Supposing that Calvin had done in France, what Wesley did in England, what a different country, in all likelihood, would France have been ! * What a different aspect would Europe have exhibited ! How different by this time, humanly speaking, would the world have been ! — We have seen what Methodism, with all its faults, has done since it began; and we have seen what reform did for the world, for two hundred years before Wesley's days. Now how came this ? Was there any material difference, in a natural and spiritual point of

* We are aware that the state of England was very different, in the days of Mr. Wesley, from the state of France, in the days of Calvin ; still, the state of the latter would be little different, in point of severity of persecution, from the state of the Roman Empire, in the days of the apostles.

view, between the two great leaders alluded to ? Strange
as the comparison may seem to some, there were certain strong features of resemblance between them.
Both were men of shrewd logical minds. Both were
men of refined taste. Both were excellent classical
scholars, and extensively acquainted with general learning. Both were men of great activity and untiring zeal.
Both were men of extended influence ; and never, perhaps, in any age of the world, have two men, during
their lives' time, and after they were gone, obtained
such an unlimited control, over the views and conduct
of their fellow-creatures. Both were, also, deeply pious.
It is true, Wesley's character is not stained with blood.
But the blot on Calvin's memory, was the stain of his
age. The gentle Cranmer might almost be said to have
thirsted for the blood of Joan Boucher, when he wrung
the warrant for her execution, from the weeping, youthful Edward. These men may be pitied, but they cannot be excused. Their own persecutions, if Christianity
did not, should have taught them not to persecute
others.

But to return ; notwithstanding the various points of
similarity between Calvin and Wesley, now enumerated,
and to which we might have added, that never were two
men more sincerely and warmly loved by their friends,
and more bitterly and mortally hated by their enemies —
they, notwithstanding, formed a very different system, in
some parts, not merely of theology, but of religious
polity. In Calvin's system, the believer and his progeny
are provided for ; but, strictly speaking, there is little
for the unbeliever. In Wesley's system, while the believer is not forgotten, in a certain way, the unbeliever
is chiefly attended to, in ministerial labour. Calvin's
pastor may, if he chuses, preach the gospel to sinners ;
but his principal business, as a pastor, is with the believers ;* and those, by him, are, generally, well instructed in the knowledge of the scriptures. Wesley's travelling

---

* See Dr. Payne on the church of Christ, page 51.

preacher makes all the artillery of the Bible tell on the consciences of the ungodly; but his class leader seldom teaches his class the oracles of God. Both systems are defective; but Wesley's has more breadth of outline in it. With all its deficiencies, it takes a more enlarged view— a more comprehensive grasp of the Christian system. This is seen, especially, in its missionary spirit. The grand characteristic of the body is, what is justly their boast, " They are *all* at work, and *always* at work."

In Calvin's system, as stated above, we see an unadaptedness to spread the gospel in the world. There was no proper provision for it. In the primitive age, there was an officer gifted and employed for the purpose. This was the evangelist. But the evangelist has scarcely any place in Calvin's system; and what little place is given him, now and then, when providence raises him up, is only in the church. He is only to be employed in bringing back Christians from antichrist, or else, to set churches in order; but this is all. He is not needed, generally, now, as the churches are all well set in order. He, also, is not needed to bring men from Baal to God, as that, in his opinion, is an employment beyond the verge of church institutions. In Wesley's system, on the other hand, the evangelist is the prominent man. His business is with the world. The unconverted are his great care. He is, also, ever enlarging the sphere of his operations. So soon as he converts some in one place, away he goes and seeks for others, in other places. Hence the rapid spread the system has made. It is, in short, adapted to spread. It is in its very nature so to do. Calvinism is chiefly adapted to spread lineally; but Wesleyanism spreads both longitudinally and latitudinally. It, in short, includes the world in its embrace.

Now, as such is the case, surely, then, it may be conceded, that the one plan is better than the other, to convert the world, and to realise all the promises and prophecies in the Bible, respecting the ultimate diffusion and influence of the Christian faith. If this be granted, our point is gained in the main; for where there is the principle of extended growth, that growth will, sooner or later, come. But this will be still more secured, the broader the basis of the missionary office is, with regard to scriptural principle. It must be acknowledged that all the missionaries that have been employed, by almost all parties, have not been so, as having any authority, that the *office* was either *commanded* in scripture, or that it had any particular *precedent* there. All the missionary zeal which has been displayed, has only proceeded from the operation of the true spirit of Christianity on the mind,—leading it to bleed over a dying world, or to perceive the obligatory and lasting character of the Saviour's commission. In consequence of this, the continued employment of missionaries will greatly depend on the ebbing and flowing of Christian feeling. But let the office have for its basis the authority of God, from legitimate, scriptural induction, and, to say the least of it, we insure for it, both a higher degree of usefulness, and a larger measure of permanence. The oak, in consequence of striking deep its roots, is more capable of resisting, either the violence of the tempest, or the scorching of the sun, than the lovely summer's flower, that speedily springs, and spreads, and buds, and blossoms, and then, suddenly, exhausts all its strength, and dies.

It is of the utmost importance, then, to the continued extension of the Redeemer's kingdom, that the principal agents employed in diffusing it should be recognised as God's agents, and not merely the agents of men; and this is adapted to have a good effect, both on missionaries, and Christians in general. With regard to missionaries, it will rescue them from the effects of enthusiasm, into which there is a danger of their plunging, by their being driven to seek their call to engage in the work from providence, rather than from the scriptures. In this point, they will be put on a level with pastors. Like them, they may, occasionally, have their misgivings, relative to their fitness for the office, but they will never have any misgivings, in respect to the office itself. A mere providential call to a providential office, might bring an individual into much distress. So long, indeed, as every thing in providence proved smooth and serene, he might feel no difficulty; but when the path began to roughen, his mind would begin to falter, and his providential call, and his providential office, would both be called in question. Place his office on a scriptural basis, and all this faltering will vanish. It will be an anchor to his soul, keeping it sure and stedfast, amidst all the turmoil — the agitations, the difficulties, and discouragements of the missionary life. It will not only prove an anchor to him, but canvas, to waft him across the ocean, when he is becalmed, and ready, it may be, to lose himself amidst the fatal shelves of indifference, or ignoble indolence.

But, putting the missionary's office on a scriptural footing, will prove not only useful to missionaries, but to Christians in general. It will do so, by evincing the imperative duty of missionary labour. We have already noticed the baneful consequences of an opposite idea, on the minds of the reformers, and, also, on nonconformists, in this country. There were no missionary societies in Dr. Owen's days. We never read of his friends, Sir Thomas Abney, or Sir John Hartopp, becoming either presidents or treasurers to any missionary societies. It is true, the gigantic missionary scheme of Cromwell was conceived in his time; and, probably, he might have been consulted in the matter, but that splendid idea was cherished more as a counterpart to the college de propaganda fide, of the court of Rome, than as a conviction that it was the duty of Christians, to send out men to preach the gospel to the heathen world. To say the least of it, it was as much a matter of policy, as of Christian zeal. Now all this arose from their views of the evangelist's office. Conscientiously, they abstained from

it as being out of the limits of church institutions.
It is, indeed, a pleasing consideration that this idea
has, comparatively, little hold of the public mind now.
It has no hold, indeed, on the majority, as far as engaging in missionary enterprise is concerned.   We
have reason to be grateful that the want of zeal for
missions is not the vice of our age.   The Catholics
need no longer taunt the Protestant church, that it
is not the church of Christ, as that church is essentially
a missionary church.   No,— Carey's Enquiry, and
Carey's example, together with the writings and ex-
amples of others, have given a new direction to the
public mind ; and if they have not refuted Dr. Owen,
they have paid little attention to his arguments.   Still,
however, there may be some who yet cling conscientiously, to the Doctor's view ; and for their sakes, and
for the sake of their assistance in the good work of
evangelizing the world, we ought to try to exhibit to
them their duty, from scripture, with regard to this
important matter.   In addition, the perception of this
idea may be the means of keeping the zeal of the
present day from flagging.   A Christian church, at
the present period, influenced by the current zeal of
the day, may send out a missionary, or missionaries,
for the conversion of the world.   But, supposing that
zeal to decline, and worldly-mindedness to gain upon
them, their support for their benevolent agents would
be liable to be withdrawn.   They would, however, still
support their pastor, from the conviction not only that
his office was a needful one, and involved in the commission of Christ, but because it was a scripturally appointed one.   Here, then, is a safe-guard to the pastoral
institution.   Let the same shield be thrown around the
missionary office, and you not only summon it into
being, but you keep it in existence.   It is then
not left to the mercy and caprice of men, or the eb-
bings and flowings of Christian piety, but a permanent
office attached to the cause of God ; and one which the

Christian public are more bound to cherish and support, by the genius of the religion they have imbibed, than to cherish and support an officer merely to edify themselves. Now what may be affirmed of one church, may equally be affirmed of many. The great leading idea of Christianity is the conversion of the world ; and next to that, the edification of the Christian church. But these ideas are apt to be reversed. They are actually so, even by many at the present day. It is this spirit that Mr. Ward so feelingly complains of, in the second of his farewell letters. It is too common, he says, to confine the Christian ministry to the building up of the church — the Christian ministry is confined to teaching, and the sublime work of preaching is laid aside. It is here, in a note, that Mr. Ward says, " the offices of apostles and prophets have ceased — but where is the next order—evangelists ? and why are pastors and teachers the only order left ?" Arising from the habit he deprecates above, Mr. Ward further says, " Hence a vast pulpit preparation is necessary, to produce incessant variety, to humour the taste of the people." " The fact is, the most of the professors in England, &c., labour under a preaching surfeit :"—" a society, say of three hundred, maintain a man to gratify them by a religious exhibition every sabbath day ; hence, three parts, out of four, of the congregations in America and England, do nothing for the conversion of the wicked in their own streets. The heathen placed fifteen thousand miles from them, are not likely, in such a state of feeling to be remembered." Now what does all this spring from ? Doubtless, from *selfishness*, as Mr. Ward justly remarks. Now selfishness is not Christianity. Christianity is the religion of self-denial, and self-denial is one of the best means of spiritual improvement — much more so than hearing a hard studied sermon got up only to please. We mean no disparagement to the pastoral office. It is one of great importance, and the person who holds it has a right to magnify his office, as well as Paul had a right to magnify his.   But no man has a right so to magnify his office as either to disparage, or set aside others.   The pastoral office has, we think, too long either subverted, or absorbed that of the evangelists.   Both of them were offices in the apostolic age, and each had its distinct duties.   They were equal in point of endowment, and equal in point of authority; for the pastor, in addressing the people of his charge, would exhort and convince, in handling the "faithful word," by the use of his extraordinary endowment, with as much authority as the evangelist would do, in addressing him and his flock, in the way either of exhorting or reproving, by the use of those inspired scriptures, that were able to make the man of God perfect, &c.   The chief difference between them was, the character of their respective labours and situations.   The one, having to superintend the converted — the other, to seek after the unconverted.   In these different departments, however, they acted with the most perfect harmony.   As they were intended by their great master, to be mutually helpful to one another, the evangelist could not do without the pastor, nor the pastor without the evangelist.   The one led the way, and the other followed.   The evangelists were like victorious chiefs, traversing and subduing one country after another; the pastors resembled the superintendants of the fortresses that had been already won.

Now all this was just as it should be; and hence, in that age, the glorious triumphs of Christianity.   We despair, however, of its full triumphs being achieved till there is a similar working, both at home and abroad, between these two important scriptural officers.   Let them be united, and the original machinery for the Christian conquest of the world, will, assuredly, not long be used in vain.   We have a miniature picture, and an earnest of all this, in the working and achievements of the travelling preachers among the Methodists, in harmony with their class leaders.   Let the different denominations of Christians, then, complete the picture, by giving it at full length. Let them, in other words, place both the institutions above referred to, on a still more scriptural footing, in order mutually to assist, but neither of them to Lord it over the other; and in our humble opinion, both the church and the world would, ere long, see a day they never saw before. The little one would then become a thousand; and the small one a strong nation. May the Lord—the Redeemer—hasten it in his time!

We have now brought our arguments for the perpetuity of the evangelist's office to a close; and from the whole, we trust, we have made good our point—that there is as much proof for the permanence of this office, as of the pastoral. We set out with the declaration that there was not a positive command for the permanence of either. The permanency of the pastoral office is gathered wholly from circumstances; it was, in consequence, said that if circumstances, equally fair, and equally numerous, could be brought forward, to establish the permanence of the evangelist's office, every candid mind must allow that permanence. We have tried to do this. We have endeavoured to shew that missionary labour, which was the essential work of the primitive evangelist, was permanent work; and, consequently involved a permanent class of such labourers. This was argued from—the genius of Christianity—the commission of Christ—the wisdom of God—and the peculiar character of the pastoral office, and other offices, in the primitive age. We then proceeded to shew that there was nothing in the work, the qualifications, call, or authority, attached to the evangelist's office, inimical to its permanence, any more than to the pastors.' After this, a number of circumstances were presented to shew, that it was our Lord's intention that the evangelist's office should be permanent. These were—the appointment of the seventy to assist his twelve disciples, which seemed to intimate that it was his will that a like class of men should hereafter assist and succeed them ;— the training of the evangelists by the apostles. after they had been endowed by our Redeemer with missionary qualification, with the apparent view to be their successors in the missionary field, when they were gone ;— the quantum of scripture employed to describe their moral qualifications and work ;— the actual committal of the missionary work into their hands, by the apostles when dying ;— and the apostles calling on them — the evangelists — to commit the same work they were called to do, to " faithful men," who should be able to teach others also ; doubtless, in the way both of assisting them, while they lived, and succeeding them when they died.

These, then, are our principal arguments for the continuity of the evangelist's office. They are so, because they are the scriptural ones. If the point cannot be proved by scripture, it cannot be proved at all. We cannot fail, however, to express our present honest conviction, that we have made out our case. We think that in the above there are inferential arguments, equally fair and numerous, that the evangelist's office was intended, by the great head of the church, to be as permanent as that of the pastor. The rest of our arguments are merely auxiliary, but we think of a kind not to be despised.— They are — The office was actually continued in the first two centuries after the apostles, as the missionaries then were styled evangelists.—The state of abeyance into which the office sunk, in the following centuries till after the reformation, arose more from moral causes in the church, than from any conviction on the minds of its members, that it was to be discontinued.— The office of the modern missionary can be regarded in no other light than either that of the legitimate station, in all that was not extraordinary, of the primitive evangelist, or else, as a human invention, to supply the deficiencies of infinite wisdom ;— and, finally, the work that still remains to be accomplished, in the

Christian conquest of the world, is one that requires the utmost *weight* to attach, not only to the *character,* but to the *office,* of those principally engaged in achieving it.

Such, then, is a summary of the arguments — scriptural and auxiliary. We wish, for the sake of the cause, they had been in better hands. Such, however, as they are, with all their imperfections — which, from a variety of circumstances, the author is conscious are many and great — they are laid before the Christian public, in the hope that, from the " signs of the times," they may meet with a more candid hearing, than they might have obtained fifty years ago.

SECTION NINTH.

Inferences from the foregoing, with concluding remarks.

From the view we have taken of the office of the primitive evangelist, in the preceding pages, the two following inferences may be drawn, namely ; the *leading design* of Christianity ; and the *means* by which that design is to be accomplished. As to the first of these, it is, as we have seen,— *the conversion of the world.* The whole New Testament proceeds upon this principle ; and the commission of Christ brings it prominently under our view. " Go into all the world, and preach the gospel to every creature : he that believeth and is baptized, shall be saved ; and he that believeth not shall be condemned." As to the means by which this design was to be effected, the following will, we apprehend, be found among the more prominent ; — the circulation of the scriptures — the employment of evangelists — the formation of individual Christian churches— and the union of all these churches. These are the principal means, and they are all in perfect harmony with the design contemplated, and are better fitted for it

o 3

than were the laws of Lycurgus, for the object he had in view, namely, the formation of warlike and patriotic Spartan citizens.

With regard to the first of these means — the circulation of the scriptures — it is one which, in every age, after the first parts of them were written, was employed for the conversion and purification of human beings. The whole Bible was completed before the end of the first century, and collected together about the middle of the second ; as we are told by Justin and Tertullian, that it was then read in the assemblies of the Christians. Ever since, it has been cherished by Christians, as the sacred depository of the doctrines they are called upon to believe, and the duties they are bound to obey. We have already noticed that it was intended to subserve the lack of those spiritual gifts in the church, which were distributed so abundantly in the apostolic age. It has been also mentioned, that the apostles and prophets had no successors — so far as being God's ambassadors, the immediate reveallers of his will to mankind, was concerned. Here they stood alone ; their office and work being both peculiar and temporary. But if they had no human successors — they were yet succeeded by their own writings ; — if they themselves could not live through every age, their writings could. "Being then dead, they yet speak." If the endowments with which they were furnished could not survive themselves, the relics of these endowments still live ; and these relics contain the substance of the word of wisdom, enjoyed by the apostles, and the gift of prophecy, enjoyed by the prophets. Thus, though the extraordinary endowments were removed from the church, there was little ground for complaint ; for what the apostle says respecting the heavenly state, is equally true respecting the church on earth, in possession of the complete canon of revelation ; "when that which is perfect is come, that which is in part" (or from parts — some, with apostles here and others with prophets there)

" shall be done away." The apostle, here, we apprehend, has this circumstance in his eye ; and illustrates the final state of blessedness by it. We think he, also, has an allusion to this, when he speaks of the church having arrived at the state of a perfect man — " the measure of the stature of the fulness of Christ" — that Christians might, in that state, no more be children, tossed to and fro, and carried about with every wind of doctrine, &c. Our Lord, too, sometimes connected near things and remote together, and illustrated the one by the other. This he did in referring to his coming to the destruction of Jerusalem, and connecting that event with his second appearance at the end of time ; and even with his coming at death to each individual ; " Be ye ready also, for in such an hour as ye think not, the son of man cometh." So, we think, in the passages above referred to, the apostle connects the idea of a perfect Bible, with a perfect man in Christ.*

In the complete canon, then, we may be said to have still the apostles with us. The important station they occupied, after the ascension of our Lord, they still fill. By their oral proclamation of divine revelation, respecting Jesus Christ as the chief corner stone of the spiritual fabric, they themselves, laid the foundation of that fabric ; and by their writings, containing the substance of the same revelation, they are still the principal means of rearing the superstructure. They are still the guides, and governors, of all inferior agents, employed in compassing their glorious design. In the carrying on of the regeneration of the world — the son of man now seated on the throne of his glory, having all power in heaven and earth given to him — has seated them on twelve thrones, that they may thus judge the twelve tribes of Israel. Here, then, is the principal means that God employs

---

* See Macknight on Eph. iv. 12-14

for carrying on his cause in the world.   Let us be grateful for it!   Let us be truly thankful that we have such a sure word of prophecy — a light to guide our feet, amidst the darkness of time, to the glories of eternity.   Let us ever dig into this mine as for hidden treasure, and make to this standard our constant appeal, in all religious controversy.   "To the law and to the testimony: if they speak not according to this word, it is because there is no light in them."   Let us all join to circulate the precious volume, throughout the habitable earth; that so it "may be filled with the knowledge of the Lord as the waters cover the sea."

Next to his word, and in connection with it, the great head of the church has employed human agency to carry on his cause in the world.   He did not, along with the Bible, communicate the invention of printing, that from Jerusalem, as a centre, it might be circulated all over the world; no, but he converted some men by his grace, and fitted them by the use of the Bible, for converting others.   Thus Peter, not the angel that was first sent to Cornelius, had to come and tell him "*words,* whereby he, and all his house, might be saved."   The *man,* and the *words* here, then, went together.   It had been so before.   When the prophets, in ancient times, were sent to the people, they carried with them the word of the Lord.   When the Levites were sent, in the days of Jehosaphat, to itinerate in Judah, it is said, "They taught in Judah, and had the book of the Law of the Lord with them; and they went throughout all the cities of Judah, and taught the people."*   The Saviour himself, as a missionary, referred to the scriptures, as well as to his own immediate revelations.   So, also, did the apostles.   They reasoned with the Jews, out of the scriptures, and when Paul went to Corinth, he went not with "the words that man's wisdom teacheth,

---

* 2 Chron. xvii. 8, 9.

but which the Holy Ghost teacheth," even the mysterious wisdom of God, in the wonderful fact of "Christ crucified." Such was the burden of the theme of the first great missionaries; and such was the theme of their assistants and successors, as missionaries, the *evangelists*. These, in compliance with the commission, carried the gospel around the world. "They went every where preaching the word." God converted them, and qualified them for this purpose; and for this purpose put them in office. "The faithful word" was committed to them for this end; and they were enjoined to "hold it fast." This they were commanded, also, to commit to other believing men, that they, after these first evangelists were gone, might teach it to others also.

It is highly probable that, on the decease of these faithful men that succeeded Timothy, as evangelists, and to whom Eusebius seems to have reference in the first of the evangelists to whom he alludes—the extraordinary endowments would terminate. This would be about the middle of the second century. We have noticed that, about the same time, the Christian canon would be collected in one volume. In this case, then, in relation, at least, to the evangelists referred to by Eusebius at the end of the second century, or the beginning of the third, the churches, instead of having the man, and the *message*, from the apostles, as in the case of Timothy, would have the man, and the *book*, as in the case of Pantænus; and as the book contained the message, where (as far as teaching truth and rebuking error was concerned) was the mighty difference between them? This, however, is the chief difference between Timothy, and all other evangelists, in every succeeding age of the world.

In this class of officers, "God our Saviour" was pleased to raise up a most important agency to carry on His cause, with relation to the great design he contemplated, the conquest of the world. The nature and stationary exercise of the only other teaching officer, connected with the church, render it absolutely necessary that such a class of officers should ever have continued, in order that, in every succeeding age, the gospel should be preached to every creature. We have referred also to the principle of common sense, as leading us to think so; and the apostle reasons, respecting this same office, on the same principle. "Whosoever," says he, "shall call on the name of the Lord shall be saved; but "how," he adds, "shall they call on him in whom they have not believed? and how shall they believe in him of whom they have not heard? and how shall they hear without a *preacher?* and how shall they preach except they be *sent?* As it is written, how beautiful are the *feet* of them that preach the gospel of peace, and *bring* glad tidings of good things! So then," he concludes, "faith cometh by hearing, and hearing by the (preaching of the) word of God." Now, this reasoning is as applicable to the state of the world at present, as when Paul uttered these expressions; and we have no doubt, if he were alive, he would utter them still; and would use his utmost efforts, with the church of God, to send out evangelists, not with messages from himself, but with Bibles in their hands, to every corner of the world.

Could we suppose, also, our Redeemer to descend to earth, what would he say to the Christians in Britain? Would he not address them in the language of rebuke, mingled with tenderness? "Oh, my friends! what have you been doing for ages? Is it not as true now, as when I sent the seventy through Palestine, that the harvest is plenteous, and the labourers few? Is it not now as necessary to pray to the Lord of the harvest, to thrust forth more labourers into his harvest? Did not I institute an office in my church, for the very purpose, and what have you made of it? Have you not kept the best of your men at home to *oversee* yourselves, and to glut your pampered appetites with splendid discourses;

and millions of your fellow-creatures, sunk in spiritual death, and hourly passing away into eternity, are living and dying destitute of instructors. Shame on such selfishness! It is true, you have begun to do a little, both at home and abroad, for the destitute and miserable; but all is little, compared with what is wanted! Go, then, and send the best of your men where they are most needed, to the region and shadow of death — the place where I myself most laboured, during my earthly sojourn; for though I shed tears over Jerusalem, I devoted most of my labours to the benighted region of Galilee."

But the evangelist is needed, not only for the spread of the gospel, but for the binding together of the churches. We have seen this was the case, in the first age, and glorious were the effects. The same is needed still; and from what we have experienced of union at home, since the cause of missions was taken up, do we not see the truth of this? And would this not be still more the case, if the evangelist's office were placed on its scriptural basis? May we not hope that it will be so ere long? May we not hope that soon the third officer will be united to the other two? Indeed, the other two are not complete without him; for without him, who shall, scripturally, ordain them? We never read of the presbytery ordaining presbyters, or bishops: no, they ordained evangelists; and the evangelists ordained them. Ordination, be it remembered, is as scriptural as election; and, therefore, the mere selection of a pastor, by a church, as some think, is not sufficient to institute a bishop or pastor to office. An important part of the will of God, in such cases, is neglected. Besides, we lose the important scriptural link that binds one church with all other churches. The evangelist is common property. He is the servant for Jesus' sake, not of one church, but all; and, therefore, he, and his fellow-labourers, tend to link all the churches together. Yes, but this, some may say, is only for newly planted, not for old established churches. It is true the mission of Titus was to the new churches in Crete, to set them in order; but when was Timothy sent to Ephesus? Macknight and others have given some very good reason to shew, that it was *after* Paul's first imprisonment at Rome.* The Ephesians had elders, when he went up to Jerusalem, before he went to Rome. Other elders, however, were needed, or, likely to be so, at Ephesus, when Timothy was left by Paul, at the time alluded to. If so, here was an evangelist at the ordination not of a first, but a second, or third bishop in a church. Their use, then, in the church, as well as the world, is for all times, and all places. Let men, then, possessing similar qualifications to Timothy, be called and ordained, as he was, and sent to perform the same duties.

Besides the scriptures and evangelists, there is, however, another means, employed by God, for the accomplishment of the object He has in view, and that is the formation of Christian churches. It is His object, in the first instance, to cure men of their spiritual maladies, and after they are cured, to keep them so. Now, in order to all this, He, in the first place, separates the cured from the diseased, and associates them together in compact bands. In these bands, they remind each other of their former diseased condition, and also of their constant need and use of the remedy provided. In order, however, that this matter may be properly attended to, He has not left it to their own prudence, but has appointed a particular class of officers, for the purpose. These officers are termed overseers; and the bands themselves are termed churches, or assemblies. When spoken of figuratively, the one party are called pastors, and the other are called flocks. This was the case in the apostolic age. The missionaries first laboured among the unconverted; and when converts were made,

---

* See Macknight's preface to 1st Epistle to Tim. Sec. 2nd.

they formed them into distinct societies. These societies, in the first instance, were instructed by the prophets and teachers of the primitive church, as in the case of the church at Antioch. Afterwards, pastors were selected from among the teachers, to take the permanent oversight of them.

Deacons seem likely to have been selected from the same class, to take especial care of the poor among them, and to be otherwise useful, that, employing the office of a deacon well, they might, as Dr. Macknight paraphrases it, " secure to themselves an honourable rank in the church, and great courage in teaching the Christian faith." Such was Stephen, and such was Philip. The remaining teachers, from whom these two classes of officers were selected, were, doubtless, employed in various ways, in using their gift — the word of knowledge — for the benefit of the community. Some, as teaching and exhorting their brethren — others, as local evangelists, from whom, in all likelihood, the future travelling evangelists would be selected. And others, would be employed, probably, in teaching the rising generation the rudiments of the Christian faith.

Here, then, appears to have been the natural order of the formation of churches, in the first ages, together with the nature of the selection of the office-bearers, and the employment of their remaining gifted men ; and such should be the case still. And such, indeed, actually is the case, to a greater or less degree, if we examine the progress of missionary undertakings. There are, first, the converts who are formed into groups, or societies ; then, in these societies, are usually found some talented men, or men, at least, with more capacity than the rest, either for thinking or speaking. From these gifted men, usually, overseers are taken, and also deacons, local preachers, sunday school teachers, and native missionaries. If we look to the operation of any missionary society, such is the usual

P

process. In different societies, there may be different names attached to different officers, but when we examine their actual use, we shall find a material similarity between them.

This is the case even at home; as instance the Methodist body. Their class leaders are not called pastors, or bishops; and yet their principal function of watching over the spiritual interests of the groups committed to their care comes very near, in its leading features, to the primitive overseer. Indeed, Mr. Wesley, as he himself expresses it, put them in that station "to overlook the rest." What is overlooking, but doing the work of an overseer, or bishop? One of the great deficiencies of this body, however, we conceive to be, the want of the recognition of this important class of labourers as the real pastors of the people — the individuals who have the charge of the converted, and not the unconverted, committed to them. But if in other communities, the pastor has usurped the office of the evangelist, it has been the contrary here. The pastoral office is here held in abeyance by the evangelist. In neither case ought such a state of things to exist. "The kings of the Gentiles," says Jesus, "exercise lordship over them, and they that exercise authority upon them are called *benefactors*. But ye shall not be so: but he that is greatest among you shall be as the younger, and he that is chief as he that doth serve, &c."— The pastor, then, must not lord it over the evangelist, nor the evangelist lord it over the pastor. They are both servants of the same Lord; and though they have different departments of service, their real business is one — the preparing men for a better world. Matters, we conceive, would very much be altered for the better, in this body, were their class leaders, or, in reality, overseers, or bishops, chosen by the people, and ordained by the evangelists, or travelling peachers, after these latter were satisfied, like Timothy, of their qualifications for the office. In addition, the

overseer should teach his spiritual charge the scriptures, as well as hear and guide their experience,
according to the injunction, " I charge you that this
epistle be read to all the holy brethren." It seems,
also, fitting that the ordinances should be administered
by these. From the strong desire we have to see
this important, zealous, and successful section of the
Christian church still more useful than they have
been, we should rejoice to observe such an alteration
among them. We fear, however, that this would not
be so easily accomplished among the old body; but
we do not see why it might not among those who
have left them, however they may be named; new
connexion — the association — or primitives. In these
bodies, both the evangelist's and pastoral office may
be put on what we conceive a truly primitive
and scriptural footing; and co-operate most harmoniously whilst endeavouring to convert the world.

We have, incidentally, somewhat digressed; but we
return to notice churches as a means of the spread
of the cause of God in the world. There are a few
things worthy of notice respecting them, viewed in this
light. The first is, the *principle of admission* into them.
The principle of admission into the primitive churches,
was not that of *seeking* salvation, but of having *found*
t. Hence, those admitted are represented as having
gladly received the word, and the " *saved ones*" — that
is, they who received peace with God through faith
in Christ, are said to have been added daily to the
church. Another thing we notice is, the *objects* of
their union. These were first; to give an exhibition of the *social* character of the Christian religion.
" By this," says the Saviour, " shall all men know that
ye are my disciples if ye have love one to another."
Secondly : to *edify one another*. See Rom. xii. 3–8.
Thirdly : the *conversion of their fellow sinners around
them*. Of the Thessalonians it is said, that not only
had the fame of their faith gone abroad; but that

from them " the word of God had sounded out into Macedonia, and even Achaia," the province bordering on it. All the capabilities of this society had, therefore, been brought into exercise on this point. Some of the gifted teachers had, doubtless, been sent out and supported by them, as evangelists, over the hills and mountains of Macedonia, rejoicing the inhabitants of the farther vales, by bringing to them glad tidings of good things. Such ought to be the case with all churches.

Mr. Ward's remarks on this subject are well worth attention. " Surely," says he, " every Christian society should consider that they are united together not for themselves, but for the extension of the kingdom of Christ. Without depending on the labours of the *evangelist* whom they maintain, the Saviour has made ample provision for the edification of his church, in the gifts of the church members, &c. Those Christians who have pleaded most strenuously for the duty of mutual exhortation, would have been in a good measure apostolical, if they had united to maintain an evangelist, to preach the gospel freely — to every creature. In this way, the apostles received aid from their brethren. But in making no provision for extending the Saviour's kingdom, and in leaving the unconverted to the bald instructions of a secular ministry, in a room apparently private, I think they have surely been mistaken."* These remarks are truly excellent. Mr. Ward makes the conversion of the world what it should be, the great business of Christians; and their own edification, however necessary, only a secondary matter. He seems, however, to have confounded the pastoral office, with that of the evangelist. He contends for the evangelist's office, when he says, the apostles and prophets have ceased, but where are the *evangelists?* and why are pastors and teachers the only order left? In the above extract, he refers to an evan-

---

* Farewell letters, pages 25, 26.

gelist being supported by a people, who may be left to edify themselves ; but makes no mention of a *pastor*, as one important means of that edification. Mr. Ward seems to forget that pastors are left, as well as *evangelists ;* and *both* are equally necessary for the well-being of the cause of Christ. In his allusions, we presume to the Scotch baptists, he seems to say, that they would in a good measure have been primitive, if they had united the maintenance of evangelists, with the rest of their church order. That order, however, includes not only exhorters, but pastors, engaged in *secular employments*, as he hints. Whether the body referred to are primitive in this latter particular, or not, we shall not attempt to determine. Perhaps the primitive pastors were self-supported in many cases, but not in others.

Dr. Bloomfield, in his notes on Acts xiv. 23, has the following remark. " At the period now in question, the presbyters probably exercised their ministry, with the trades, or professions, to which they had been brought up." If the pastors of that time, were employed in business, the unconverted were not, however, left to their " bald instructions ; no, the evangelists — supported by God's law, 1 Cor. ix. 14. — had the care of them ; and when they converted any, they handed them over, for further instruction, to the kind of pastors alluded to. The parties, then, on whom Mr. Ward animadverts, would not be far, according to his own acknowledgement, from being truly primitive — if to their *secular ministry*, in the meetings of their church members, they added the support of evangelists, wholly devoted to the work. This they might do, as churches, or else as a denomination ; appointing evangelists to separate districts, all over the country, where, like the original home missionaries, the seventy, they could, two and two, proclaim divine mercy to all around them.

Such, then, are some of the advantages to the cause of God, resulting from the formation of particular Christian societies. But we shall proceed to consider the other means that God has appointed for this end; namely, the *union* of all these churches.

It was noticed, in the first part of this little work, that the first churches were both independent and united. They were independent, in the admission and expulsion of members; in the choice of their office bearers; and, also, in the controul of their contributions. They were united, in their recognition of each other as Christian churches; in their mutual advice, and sympathies; and, also, in their co-operation, in the furtherance of every important object, connected with the establishment and progress of Christianity. This union was based on their mutual views, feelings, and prospects, arising from their connection with Christ. He was head of that body which, as a whole, they formed. The object of this union is finely expressed by the apostle. Eph. iv. 8-16. There, he affirms, that Christ ascended on high, and gave gifts to man. In the Psalm cited, it is said, "Thou hast received gifts for men, yea, for the rebellious also, that the Lord God might dwel among them." That God might dwell, then, with rebellious men, was the object of the bestowment of the Saviour's gifts. These gifts were apostles, prophets, evangelists, pastors, and teachers. Hence it is said, they were given for the perfecting, or organizing, or joining together (Καταρτισμον) of those thus made holy ones; though formerly in a state of enmity to each other, as well as in a state of rebellion against God. Of this, these Ephesians, themselves, had been remarkable instances, as stated ch. ii. 11-19. They had been, formerly, aliens from, but were then incorporated with, the church of God.

Now, this jointing together of penitent believing Jews and Gentiles, as a body, was with a view towards a further object, namely, *the work of the ministry*. This is usually supposed to refer to those who, in modern times, are termed ministers; but we rather imagine the apostle has in view, the general working of all the parts of the body of Christ. To the same idea he elsewhere refers, when he speaks of the operation of eyes, and ears, and hands, and feet, as all assisting and contributing to one result — the benefit of the body in general. So in the present passage, this work of the ministry is, " in order to (*us*) the *edifying* of the body of Christ;" or, as more fully expressed in the sixteenth verse — " From whom (Christ) the whole body fitly joined together, and compacted by that which *every joint* supplieth, according to the effectual working in the measure of *every part*, maketh increase of the body, unto the edifying of itself in love." Now, all this working of every part, for the good of the whole body, is, we are told, to proceed till " *We all* (the whole redeemed body of Christ, we apprehend, in all ages) come, in the unity of the faith, or by a like faith, and knowledge of the son of God, unto a perfect man" — or complete body — " unto the measure of the stature of the fulness of Christ."

Here, then, we have the object of the union of the church, as a whole (for it is not one church the apostle is here speaking of), and what is that object but the great leading design of Christianity, the conversion of the world? — the gathering all true believers, in all climes, and in all ages, to be to the praise of the riches of the grace of God in the heavenly world. To this object, all the energies of the Christian world ought to be directed. The talents, the influence, and the property, of Christians, ought to run into this channel. They did so in the primitive age; and they ought to do so still. The circulation of the scriptures, then, and the employment and support of suitably qualified evangelists, both at home and abroad, ought to be their untiring aim. As to their own personal comfort and edification, every true hearted man will be of Mr. Ward's mind; he will either try to edify himself, or be content with the feebler edification of some others, rather than detain a faithful minister of Christ, fitted to be extensively useful, always in one place, to please him. Yes! he will gladly resign his pastor, in order to be more generally useful, as does the good man in a place of worship, when he resigns his seat in his pew, to a timid stranger, in the hope that he may receive benefit to his immortal soul, by his visit to a place of worship. In acting on this principle, he will find he is making the best use of the means of grace. A Christian never obtains more good to himself, than when he is doing good to others. "He that watereth, shall be watered also himself." "They shall prosper that love thee." Never did Britain flourish more, in a spiritual point of view, than since her sons began to feel for the heathen world.

But how is this union to be effected? By meeting all denominations, as much as possible, on common ground. The Bible Society and Tract Society exhibit instances of this; and so, likewise, the general prayer meeting, at the commencement of the May meetings in London. Nothing is more adapted to do good to the world than such unions as these. They seem like the answer of the Redeemer's prayer, "that all his children might be one, that the world might know that the Father had sent him."

A general union, however, among all denominations, can only, at present, be effected, in a very partial way. Denominations may, however, unite, and sections of denominations may do so, with a view to spread the gospel, both at home and abroad. This has been effected, in several denominations, and with very happy results. Strange, however, as it may seem, there are some excellent individuals, and even churches, that are very jealous on the score of union. They read and hear of its abuse among certain parties, and this induces them to oppose the *principle* itself, as bad. But surely, these parties need not be told that lawful use is one thing, and unlawful abuse another. There is nothing connected with Christianity, that has not been

abused ; so that, if we are to abstain from one thing,
because it has been abused, we may, equally, abstain
from all. We conceive that the *unity* of *a number of
churches*, and even *a whole denomination*, may exist,
without the *least infringement of the independence* of any
one of them, on the *points* in which the first churches
were independent. Not one of them lost its liberty, in
these points, by asking advice respecting the will of God,
in a particular matter, of the apostles, and the church at
Jerusalem. Not one of them lost its independence, by
joining with a number of others in a common object —
the relief of the poor saints at Jerusalem ; and by choos-
ing messengers to carry that relief. Neither the church
at Philippi, or Thessalonica, or Berea, or any other
church in Macedonia, lost its individual control of its
contributions, or any other point of legitimate independence, in sending contributions to the support of Paul,
at Corinth.

Some churches, it is true, at that period, appear to
have been very shy of such unions; but this did not
redound much to their credit ; hence says Paul to the
Philippians, " No church communicated with me, as concerning giving and receiving, but ye only." Now, this
was saying little for these churches. They were as
much indebted to the Redeemer as the Philippians ; and,
therefore, ought to have equally united to have supported his servant, in preaching the gospel, as they did.
The fact is, there is reason to fear, with regard to some,
opposed to the principle of union, that this opposition
arises as much from jealousy of their own importance, as
of the purity of Christianity. It has been remarked
that, in the first age, the evangelists were, under
the Redeemer, not only the great means of converting
the world, but of uniting the church ; but none at that
period, opposed them so much as Diotrephes, who *loved
to have the preeminence.* It is said, he received not the
brethren who went forth preaching the gospel, taking
nothing of the Gentiles, — but cast out of the church

such as did. As nations have, in politics, to beware as much of the tyranny of an oligarchy, as of a monarchy, so, in religion, the churches of God have as much to beware of the tyranny of many popes, in individual churches, as of the tyranny of one over many.

The precise point where Christian union in combination with Christian liberty ends, and antichristian tyranny begins, may be a problem difficult to solve speculatively. The timid and over scrupulous minds of some, would keep it *within* its proper and useful limits; and the sanguine and ardent temperaments of others, would extend it *beyond* the boundary where a proper check could be given to the aggressions of ecclesiastical domination. The medium point between the two, then, is, most likely, *that where combined usefulness and individual safety can operate harmoniously.* This point may, perhaps, be ascertained, by exemplifying the union of the two following states of mind: First, a hearty determination to co-operate with others, in all that is good and useful to man, and tending to the glory of God. And second, a stern resolve to resist every attempt at control, by the imposition of impertinent, unjust, or unscriptural laws, with regard to either faith or practice.

The first of these states of mind is involved in the possession of Christianity itself; for as Christianity imparts an adhesive principle, to all who enjoy it, and leads them to coalesce with others in Christian fellowship, saying, "let them that fear thee turn unto me." "I am a companion of all them that fear thee;" so societies, composed of such persons, must be inclined to adhere to other societies of like individuals;— and as there is no promise in the Bible to any person, in his individual capacity, but as connected with others, so there is no promise to particular churches, unless as combined with the general church, in helping forward the cause of God throughout the world. Dr. Owen's observations on this subject, are well worth attention. "No church" says he, "is so independent as that it can always, and in all cases, observe the duties it owes unto the Lord Christ and the church Catholic, by all those powers which it is able to act in itself distinctly, without conjunction with others; and that church which confines its duty unto the acts of its own assemblies, cuts itself off from the external communion of the church Catholic: nor will it be safe for any man to commit the conduct of his soul to such a church."* No church, therefore, can be regarded as holding just and scriptural views upon the subject of Christian union, which is prevented from associating with others, from the fear that that association may lead to abuse.

On the other hand, with regard to the other state of mind, it seems one equally necessary. Association has been abused, and it may be so again. So, however, as already noticed, has every thing connected with the kingdom of Christ; but as this should not prevent us attending to those things that have been abused, so it should induce us equally to be on our guard, against every real manifestation of abuse. Whenever an association, or a union, or a conference, erects a jurisdiction incompatible with the laws of Christ, and the rights and liberties of individual societies, it is the duty of these societies to resist it. It is true that a number of churches may have the power of reproving one when guilty of offence, as that church has power to reprove one of its members for doing wrong. No individual, when he joins a Christian society, thereby resigns his personal liberty of judging and acting for himself; but, notwithstanding this, when he becomes connected with that society, he must expect, from that very union, to be corrected when he does wrong; and, if he maintains a Christian frame of mind, he will be thankful for this; he will say "Let the righteous

---

* On the true nature of a gospel church, chap. xi. on the communion of churches.

smite me, it shall be a kindness, yea, I shall esteem it
an excellent oil, that will not break my head, and my
prayer also shall be for him in the day of his calamity."
Similar will be the feeling of a right hearted Christian
society, in relation to the reproofs of other societies,
when it does wrong. Instead of spurning, it will
gladly receive reproof; and the society that acts
otherwise, is unworthy the name of a Christian church.
So, also, is the society that will quietly bow its neck,
to receive the yoke of an unchristian association — an
association where that mystery of iniquity — that bane
of all that is useful in the church of God — prevails,
namely, ecclesiastical tyranny. Submission here, is
degradation — is slavery of the meanest character — it
is not submission to heaven, it is submission to hell.
Communion here, is not the communion of saints, but
the communion of demons; and "what fellowship hath
righteousness with unrighteousness? And what communion hath light with darkness, and what concord
hath Christ with Belial? or what part hath he that
believeth with an infidel? And what agreement hath
the temple of God with idols?—Wherefore come out
from among them, and be ye separate, saith the Lord,
and touch not the unclean thing, and I will receive
you." Here, then, is the duty of all Christians, indi-
vidually and socially, with regard to what is evil, either
in the world, or, in the church. Separation, when
there cannot be cordial co-operation on Christian principle, is not sin, but duty. Hence, say the scriptures,
"come out of her my people, that ye be not partakers of
her sins, and that ye receive not of her plagues."—
Schism, here, is not the rending of the body of Christ,
but the rescue of that body from a degraded and danger-
ous position.

Here, then, appear to be the medium feeling, and,
perhaps, the scriptural line of conduct, between the undue
fear of evil, on the one hand, and the over sanguine
expectation of good, on the other, in regard to the

association of Christian churches. Unlike the one, it never says, "there is a lion in the streets;" no, it courageously presses onward, fearless of evil, till evil is seen: and unlike the other, when this evil actually appears, and the hope of good is for ever fled, it gradually beats its retreat, and reluctantly retires into solitude, with a heart bleeding over the miseries of man, owing to the degraded and useless character of many connected with the professing church of Christ.

On the whole, then, these two principles — the unity and independency of the churches — ought ever to go hand in hand, acting harmoniously; and neither should be allowed to lord it over the other. If it is so, evil must, inevitably, ensue to the cause of God in the regeneration of the world. If independency is allowed to triumph over unity — all that is cold, and isolating, and repulsive, will, most certainly, follow. Schism, that baleful evil, will appear in all its hideous deformity, rending, and mangling, and scattering the body of Christ, to the four winds of heaven; exhibiting a spectacle so appalling, as to excite, and call forth, at once, in affecting combination, the shriek of the good, and the triumph of the wicked. If, on the other hand, unity is allowed to triumph over independency, all that is sacred in the rights of conscience — all that is dear to man in the name of liberty, — is gone. The name will belie the thing.— The semblance of love, will be the reality of hate; and, the associating principle, intended to give an exhibition of the sacred concord of heaven, will yield only a striking likeness of the guilty conspiracy of hell. To dethrone God was the combined effort of the devil and his angels; and to dethrone God and occupy his place, even in his own church, has been the combined effort, frequently, of an ambitious and rapacious priesthood, represented in scripture under the name of "the man of sin," by crushing the liberties,

Q

and chaining the consciences, of those whom they called the church Catholic on earth.

From the foregoing remarks, it will be easily inferred, to what extent our admiration of the system of Mr. Wesley is carried. We are the warm admirers of its missionary character. We sincerely think it most primitive, with regard to its travelling preachers. In these, we think, we see the nearest approximation to the primitive evangelists, of any party of Christians that we know of. Still, we think, that, in the system, taken as a whole, there is much room for emendation, on several important points. We have already mentioned one, and that not the least, namely, the improvement of which the office of class leader is susceptible. But there is another, and that is, the want of the recognition of distinct, independent, societies. Here, we think, the scheme a failure, as it regards a reflection of the churches in the early ages. We think we have given pretty clear evidence that these churches were independent in four points — the reception of their members — the expulsion of their members — the election of their office-bearers — and the control of their contributions; but, so far as we know, we think there is the absence of these, in individual methodist societies. We strongly suspect the evangelists take more upon them, in all these points, than Timothy either did, or was enjoined to do. We may be wrong; and if so, we shall be glad to be corrected.

But the worst feature of the whole system is, the evangelists taking the whole power of managing the concerns of the body, into their own hands. The Conference, we are told, is composed of the preachers only. No representatives of the people are admitted there; and every thing approaching to democracy is said to be hated. Now, if all this be true, we are sorry for it, for we think we see something like democracy running through the whole of the New Testament. Even the apostles themselves, did nothing without the people. They did not even announce the mind of the Spirit to the Syrian churches, without the voice of the people. See Acts xv. 22. They did not elect a fellow apostle, without the multitude. They did not choose deacons, without the multitude of the disciples; and the bishops and deacons of all the churches were to be proved by the disciples, before Timothy, or any other evangelist, was called to lay his hands on them. They also made no demand for money. They gave orders, indeed, how it might be collected, if the people were willing to give it. They, also, never controled evangelists in the way of making them go, by their authority, to any particular place. They solicited, but never demanded. See the case of Paul with Apollos, I Cor. xvi. 12. Surely, then, all this shews that the apostles had less dread of democracy, than many in modern times.—— They did nothing without the people. Now, though we believe that, in the main, the ministers of the Wesleyan body have endeavoured to use the power they enjoy, by the will of their founder, and their own custom, to the advancement of the cause of God, both at home and abroad, yet we should rejoice to see them adopt a more scriptural standard; being assured that, sooner or later, every thing that is in opposition to such a standard, will meet with its just reward. It will be "consumed by the spirit of the Lord's mouth, and destroyed by the brightness of his coming."

From the preceding remarks, it will also be seen, that we have no sympathy with the philippic of Mr. Beverly, against the Congregational Union. On the contrary, we heartily agree with that and similar unions among the congregational body — baptist and pædobaptist. We fondly hope that such unions will be so conducted, as to shew that the unity of many churches is perfectly compatible with their individual independency. As this section of the Christian church is already renowned in British story, for the union of power and toleration, in a higher degree than had been shewn by others, so, we trust, it will not only maintain, but improve its character, as the stern asserter of individual liberty, in connexion with all that gentleness and amiability, that lead us to unite with all, in the way of rejoicing with them that do rejoice, and weeping with them that weep ; and, above all, in the way of doing good : in promoting the glory of God, and the eternal interests of all mankind.

But we must now draw to a conclusion, as we fear that, by this time, we shall have exhausted the patience of our readers. We only wish, then, farther to say, that what is written in the preceding pages, has been so, whether right or wrong, with the best intentions ; and is now respectfully submitted to the candid consideration of Christians of all denominations, not for the purpose of collecting from among them a new sect, but with the friendly view, if possible, of benefitting all. It is natural, indeed, for all parties to suppose that at present, they are as well as they either can, or need be. This is the case, especially, with the bigotted and indolent. At the present period, however, there is a spirit of enquiry abroad, among many of almost all denominations, that will not be satisfied with the authority that arises, either from antiquity, or from great names. It must, indeed, be confessed, that among these, are to be found not a few restless spirits, that will not be satisfied with any thing. But such has been the case, at all times, under similar circumstances. At the reformation, when the spirit of free enquiry came over Europe, after a long night of slumber in the lap of the church of Rome, a mighty reaction set in ; and, in consequence, many, with the quickest velocity, ran from one extreme to another : from the extreme of taking every thing for granted, to the opposite extreme of being governed by nothing — not even the word of God itself. The word of man, was all that was needful, at one time ; but the word of God was not sufficient for these persons then. But if this was the case with some, it was not the case with all. A goodly number were led, most materially to improve their former creed. A considerable portion of the precious grain of divine truth was acquired, by such persons, though this was still in connexion with some of the chaff with which it was mixed. This chaff, however, required to be blown away; and in the case of some, it was so, in a good degree. Others, however, retained it more tenaciously; and hence the polemical warfare that ensued among protestants. That warfare continues to the present day. It is now carried on as keenly as ever, if not so fiercely, as in by gone days. Agitation, in one form or other, is, indeed, one of the distinguishing signs of our own times. The political world is full of it, and so is the religious. Almost all parties, more or less, are agitated by questions of reform. The Catholics have their reformers; the church of England hers; and the different parties among the Dissenters have theirs. It is, indeed, a winnowing time. The Redeemer seems to have arisen with the fan in his hand, "thoroughly to purge his floor, to gather the wheat into the garner, and to burn up the chaff with unquenchable fire."

Amidst all this, then, an important question naturally arises, namely, how should such a spirit be met? We answer, not by inflammatory publications, nor by crude or ill concocted theories, but by calm, and dispassionate discussion, of what appears to be the will of God, in the scriptures, on any particular subject. Such, especially, ought to be the case, with every thing that relates to the leading design of Christianity, and the means to carry that into execution, lest all our working should be thrown away on an improper object; or, though the object be ever so worthy, lest we should, through our ignorance of the right means, prevent ourselves from attaining it. And, surely, what is revealed in scripture, upon these important points, cannot be so obscure, as many suppose; and, perhaps, it only

Q 3

requires an unbiased state of mind, for all parties to come nearly to the same conclusion respecting them. It were, indeed, a libel on eternal wisdom, to suppose it to be otherwise. It is matter of deep regret, that many moral causes are still at work, with many among all parties, to prevent their bowing to the plain and obvious dictates of that wisdom. There is much reason to fear that the *interests* of many, and the *prejudices* of more, tend to darken the clearness of its light. As unity among Christians, however, is a desirable object, both for the sake of Christianity, and the conversion of the world, every Christian ought to be on his guard against the influence of any bias; and to direct his inquiries, with the utmost simplicity of intention, in order to ascertain the mind of the spirit, as revealed in the scriptures. This ought, especially, to be the case, with every one who takes on him the character of an instructor, or a reformer. In addition, however, to simplicity of intention, such an one ought to exert the greatest care in " comparing spiritual things with spiritual." He ought to take a leaf out of the book of the philosopher, in acting on the principle of cautious patient induction : and when he has done his utmost in this way, when laying his lucubrations before the world, while he may express his own present convictions with firmness, he ought, if he wishes to do good, to avoid every thing approaching to dogmatism. The sword of the spirit has often been blunted by the violence of the heart, as well as the unskilfulness of the arm of him that has attempted to wield it. Every attempt at reform, conducted in such a way, must, inevitably, prove a failure.

It would, indeed, be the highest presumption for the writer of the preceding pages, to suppose that he can, in almost any degree, influence public opinion. His ability, he is convinced, is too small; his influence too limited; and the circle of his acquaintance too narrow, ever to allow him to entertain such an idea. His present attempt, therefore, is intended chiefly to benefit, if he possibly can, the limited range of the small circle in which he moves. He rejoices, however, to have to say that, within that circle, small as it is, he can number some of all the leading denominations in the kingdom. He has the hope that some of these will listen to what he has to say; but it is only by his acting in the spirit, and in the manner he would recommend to others, that he can expect, in any degree, to influence even their opinions. He has, therefore, endeavoured to act, to the utmost of his power, on the principle of patient, scriptural induction. He has expressed his own conclusions, with all the firmness of honest conviction; but he trusts, that he has done so, in such a way, as not to offend those who may think differently. In all that he has said, respecting the leading design of Christianity, and the machinery to carry that design into execution, it may, however, be affirmed, that he has said nothing new; as all, if not speculatively received, is yet acted upon, more or less, by all the leading denominations in the country. This, he allows, so far, to be true; but still, if the view which he has taken of the evangelist's office were admitted, it might affect present arrangements, among all parties, to a greater or lesser degree. Missionaries are, indeed, employed, both at home and abroad; but they are so, rather as an expedient of pious zeal, than as officers founded on scriptural authority. Dr. Owen's objections to the erection of such an office as theirs still remain, in all their force, on the minds of many. It has no prototype in the New Testament; it is " beyond the verge of church institutions." So long as this idea prevails, the missionary, so far as his spiritual engagements are concerned, will be entirely moulded by those who employ him. They cannot be expected to enquire, as is done in the case of the pastoral office, what are the scriptural duties required of him; as the duties of such an officer are, on their hypothesis, nowhere prescribed.

If the evangelist's office, however, be allowed, from scriptural authority, to be permanent in the church, then matters may be somewhat altered. The office of missionary, in all its great outlines especially, must be regulated by the directions of inspired truth; and not by the prudence, or the caprice, of pious, and well-intentioned men. Let the present view, then, respecting the missionary's office, be altered, and such alteration could not fail to be the signal of alteration, not only of the institution itself, but, to a greater or less degree, of kindred institutions, connected with the various parties now in existence. In some of these, it would tend to alter the name, and regulate, and greatly increase the work of the *present bishop*. To ordination and confirmation he, as an evangelist, in company with a suitable companion, would have frequently to traverse what might be termed his diocese, in preaching the gospel, in order to the conversion of sinners, and in planting and watering new churches, and ordaining bishops and deacons over them. Other communities, also, would have to expand their present views and doings, and, perhaps, in some respects, to make some slight alterations. Pastoral work would be confined within the sphere of its legitimate duties in the church; and evangelists would be called forth, to preach the gospel to the world. Those disposed and fitted for foreign service, would be sent to that service; and those disposed and fitted for home service, would be sent to it. These latter, might be attached to particular churches in towns, where they might preach to sinners; and, also, in extensive districts around. In the villages, small churches might be formed; and these placed under the care of suitable overseers, adapted to their present state.

A considerable approximation to all this, is, at present, to be seen in many churches, in different parts of the country. The carrying of it out, then, perhaps, is only wanted, in order to make our native land, in a spiritual point of view, to rejoice and blossom as the rose: and what is adapted to do good to this country, is equally adapted to do good to all others.

If the views which have been contended for are right, then a partial, if not an organic change would take place in some other communities. These are they in which, at present, the evangelist's office exhibits more of its primitive aspect, than in most others. If the evangelist's office is found in abeyance in other communities, the pastoral office is found in abeyance here. Here, then, this circumstance will be corrected: the class leader will be installed in the office of the primitive overseer, and, consequently, be called to the performance of the duties peculiar to his sta'ion. If the above views are correct, and be adopted, it will also follow, that union will be a prominent matter, in all the churches. All will strive together for the faith of the gospel; and nothing will more contribute to this, than the support of an ambulatory class of labourers. Doing this, even under present circumstances, has contributed, most materially, to the union that, at present, exists. How much more would this be the case, were the office of missionary placed on a more scriptural footing? And, finally, this would more likely be realised, by avoiding, in connexion with this union, every thing like compulsion, with regard to individual societies. In the religion of the New Testament, the heart is every thing. If this is right, every thing will be easy, as far as Christian association is concerned; the hand will be open, and the purse will be open likewise; but let us act on the principle of compulsion, and we shut both. The history of the church, in all ages, attests the truth of this. It is, doubtless, with a view to prevent all jarring among the churches of Christ, that their great head has established among them the two principles of liberty and unity — the liberty of each, and the unity of all. Opposing as these two principles may appear to be, we may rest assured, that their individuality and combina_ tion, are alike worthy of that Being whose wisdom and goodness have constituted all the arrangements of his church, as well as the arrangements of nature. As the seemingly discordant principles of attraction and repulsion bind together the various parts of the material universe, so, in like manner, the seemingly opposing principles of liberty and unity, are intended to bind together, during their continuance on earth, the various parts of the church of the living God.

Such, then, would be some of the effects arising from the operation of the principles presented in the preceding pages, on the supposition of their being adopted, by different parties, as scriptural. Without the view of leading to the formation of a new denomination, if acted upon by each at present in existence, they would all, ere long, make a gradual approximation to one another. By one party dropping what is redundant, and another supplying what is defective, the watchmen in each would soon begin to see eye to eye. And would not this be desirable? Would not this be a consummation most devoutly to be wished for? O surely! The dawn of such a day, would be the dawn of that day so much desired, and so long anticipated — the day of our Redeemer s reign, — the millennial day, — the day when all the glowing visions of the Hebrew and Christian prophets shall be realized, in all their glory and splendour. To help forward such a day, ought, surely, to be the study and aim of every Christian — of every church — of every denomination. Such, especially, ought to be the study and aim of every one who attempts to write on Christian subjects, and, particularly, those which relate to the machinery that God himself has put in motion, for the recovery of a lost world. Every wheel of that machinery ought to be carefully sought for, and all of them carefully put together, each in its respective place; that nowhere there may be found any friction, but that the whole may work harmoniously. Such has been the object of the writer of these pages, so far as he knows his own heart. If, however, he should discover, eventually, that he has been mistaken in his views, he shall regret that he has troubled any portion of his fellow-creatures with any of his own vain speculations; yet, he trusts, he shall cheerfully acquiesce in the decision against him, so soon as he shall see cause to confess his error. But if, on the contrary, he should, eventually, in the estimation of the Christian public, prove to be correct, he shall certainly be grateful to the Father of lights, for enabling him, in any measure, to be the instrument of assisting the information of his people, and of quickening their zeal, in relation to His own sacred cause. To the blessing of God then, and to the careful and candid perusal of his readers, he commends this his humble effort.

THE END.

T. H. Clark, Printer, Newgate Street, Newcastle.

Date Loaned

MAY 3 1950			

Demco 292-5

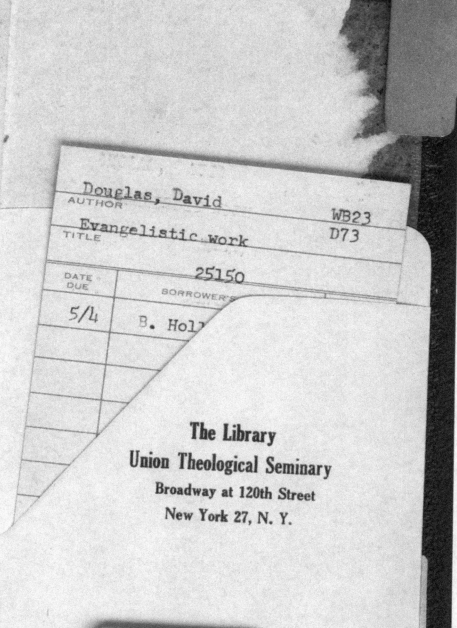

Check Out More Titles From HardPress Classics Series In this collection we are offering thousands of classic and hard to find books. This series spans a vast array of subjects — so you are bound to find something of interest to enjoy reading and learning about.

Subjects:
Architecture
Art
Biography & Autobiography
Body, Mind &Spirit
Children & Young Adult
Dramas
Education
Fiction
History
Language Arts & Disciplines
Law
Literary Collections
Music
Poetry
Psychology
Science
…and many more.

Visit us at www.hardpress.net